Change Forward

Change Forward

*Maximize Change To Take Your
Life Forward*

Jeff Daws

Edited by Joe Oliver

XULON PRESS

Xulon Press
2301 Lucien Way #415
Maitland, FL 32751
407.339.4217
www.xulonpress.com

Paperback ISBN-13: 978-1-6628-2714-3

Ebook ISBN-13: 978-1-6628-2715-0

Contents

Dedication

I dedicate this book to my mentor and friend Dr. Benny Tate. Pastor Benny, this book is all about change, and if anyone has challenged me to change, it's been you. You've taught me more by your actions than your words. Your love for people has taught me to find ways to make people feel valued and loved. Your generous actions have moved me to be a more generous person and pastor. Your actions have taught me to be generous to missionaries across the ocean and to be generous to the church down the street. You have taught me to look for ways to encourage every person I come in contact with. You have taught me to think bigger with God. You have allowed Rhonda and me to be a part of your and Barbara's life, and for that I am forever grateful. This God-connection with you has given me a new direction in life and ministry. My life has changed for the better in order to give people an opportunity for a better life in Jesus Christ. Thank you, Pastor Benny, for the investment you have made in me. All who read this book will benefit from your investment in me. I love and appreciate you more than words can say.

Acknowledgments

I want to thank my wife, Rhonda Daws, for her insights that are a part of this book. I also send out thanks to Emmalyn Roell, Chesnee Dorsey, and Joe Oliver for all of their ideas and feedback as I worked on this book. I'm so grateful for their input and wisdom. They helped me take this book to the next level. And I want to say a special thank you to everyone who was willing to share their story of challenge, setback, and ultimate victory in this book. My prayer is that many lives will be touched and changed by their testimony that God has the final say in everything.

Chapter 1

Before Anything Gets Better

The wind howled fiercely around the climber as he reached up and felt along the frozen, rocky surface of the mountainside. Pellets of snow and ice stung his face. He could feel the cold creeping into his body. He looked down at the safety rope wrapped around his waist. Aside from his feet and fingers gripping tiny crevices in the rock, that rope was the only thing keeping him from plummeting 27,000 feet to the ground far below.

The wind picked up, buffeting his body. He could feel his aching fingers losing strength. He stared up, trying to peer through the clouds swirling around him. "How far away am I from the top?" he wondered.

He glanced below to check on his teammate, but he couldn't see them. As far as he knew at that moment, it was just him, God, and the mountain. His mind wandered back to all the newspaper reports he had read over the years of other climbers who had tried to conquer the mountain, only to fail. Some never returned, their bodies lost somewhere on the mountain's frozen peaks.

Suddenly, the dark clouds above split, and he caught a glimpse of his ultimate goal: the mountain top!

Though everything in his body wanted to stop and turn back, a surge of renewed determination jarred his mind from its dark thoughts. He gritted his teeth and commanded his arms to extend again. "I will not let this mountain defeat me!" he snarled under his breath. "I *will* conquer this mountain! It will *not* conquer me!"

And with each slow, painful move, Sir Edmund Hillary and his teammate Tenzing Norgay climbed the remaining 2,000 feet to the summit, to become the first people to ever reach the top of Mt. Everest.

———————

Today, mountain climbers still attempt to conquer Mt. Everest's towering heights and quickly discover why so few have made it to the top. A few make it, but many fail and have to turn back. And just like in Sir Edmund Hillary's day, some lose their lives to the mountain's dangers.

George Mallory was one of these people. In the early 1920s, he tried several times to scale Mt. Everest but had to turn back. He tried one more time, telling his friends, "I can't see myself coming down defeated," before starting his long and exhausting trek back up the rocky giant. However, despite his determination and experience, Mallory disappeared on its snowy slopes.

Concerned for his well-being and for the success of the mission, his teammates anxiously waited for his return at the camp below. After much time passed, they finally accepted that the mission had failed and sadly packed up the camp and returned to England. Later attending a banquet honoring Mallory, it is said that when the attendees applauded the team's chief, he stood, with tears in his eyes, and pointed at a painting of Mt. Everest hanging on the wall behind him. With fierce determination, he declared to the mountain, "You defeated us once; you defeated us twice. You defeated us three times. But we shall someday defeat you, because you can't get any bigger but we can!"

Three decades later, Sir Edmund Hillary fulfilled this promise. But this is not where the story of George Mallory ends.

In 1999, climbers found Mallory's missing body. It had been amazingly preserved by the snow and ice and proclaimed to the world a testimony of determination. His frozen arms were extended overhead, fingers tensed to hold onto the rock face, his feet pointed to find support. Even in the last moments of his life, Mallory refused to give up and fought on to achieve his goal.

It's Possible

What might seem impossible to change in your life today may be possible in your future *if* you start climbing today. Like the stories of these mountain climbers from the past, it's highly unlikely that you can change the mountains you face in your life. They're mountains after all: huge, unmoving obstacles that seem undefeatable.

But I do have great news for you. Even though you can't change the mountain, you can change *yourself.* You can grow and get better, day by day, until you are strong enough to conquer your mountains' heights.

Not every mountain is the same height, and, in the same way, some mountains in your life will be easier to conquer. Others will take much more time and effort on your part to overcome.

I've written this book to share with you some of the tips and techniques that have helped me to scale to the top of some of the biggest challenges in my life. Along the way, I've learned that if I ever want to conquer any of life's mountains, I must grow myself.

I'd like to take you on a journey now and share with you some of the wisdom I've learned from my mistakes and from the mistakes of others. Join me as we scale the heights of life's challenges to find that we *can* change and overcome!

The Blame Game

It is natural to believe that the people and situations around us are responsible to change us or at least make our lives better without any effort of our own. Many times, instead of taking charge of our lives and the decisions we make, it's really easy to just sit back and coast along through life. And this may even work for a while, especially if things seem to go our way.

But what happens when we get stuck?

I've been tubing at Deep Creek in North Carolina many times in my life. If there's been a lot of rain, the water is high, and tubers float along quickly. But if there hasn't been rain for a while, the water level is low, and tubers frequently get stuck on rocks.

That's the picture I want you to see in your mind throughout this book, because there are millions and millions of people right now who are stuck on the rocks of life. But instead of standing up, picking up their inner tube, and walking to where the water is deeper, they just STAY THERE, expecting someone else to rescue them.

To me, it's become an alarming part of modern American culture to expect someone to bail us out. And let me be clear here that I'm not talking about something awful happening in our lives or about God answering our prayers by providing a desperately needed blessing. I'm talking about people who *continuously live* expecting others to rescue them.

And if no one rescues them, this is when the Blame Game starts. They blame their parents. They blame their teachers. They blame their co-workers, employers, the government, big business, their neighbors, the church, God...ANYONE. If I had a dollar for every time that I heard someone say, "It's their fault that my life's a mess," I'd be rich!

Waiting for other people to rescue you will keep you paralyzed and stuck in life. You may have felt like this before in your life. You may feel like it now.

In order to move forward, we have to stop fixing the blame and start fixing the problem. A failure can be overcome, but an excuse removes the power to rise up above the problem.

Here's a valuable nugget of hope for you: When you take on the spirit of responsibility and stop blaming others for what they did to you or what they didn't do for you, you'll start to grow as a person and eventually become bigger than your problems.

Help My Daughter

Several years ago, when my sister was enduring a painful divorce, her daughter was around five years old. Despite trying everything she could to save her marriage, my sister finally conceded that the relationship was over. Her mind went to how this decision would impact her daughter, and so she asked me what she could do to help her little girl.

At the time, I didn't have an immediate response. So I started doing research on the effect of divorce on children. Somewhere in my readings, I ran across the statement, "If the parents get better, the children will be alright." I keyed in on this: The *parents* had to get better *first*. If the parents get help and begin the healing process, their children will also get better.

When I went back to my sister with this information, she seemed a bit skeptical at first. But as she worked on her life after divorce, she saw an improvement in her daughter's outlook as well.

In order for any of us to improve our lives, we have to change.

Change How We See Things

At the time of writing this book, I've been the lead pastor of Stockbridge Community Church for twenty-five years. One of the greatest privileges I have as a pastor is to see people accept Jesus as their Savior and start their daily walk with serving God.

In their lives, change starts on the inside and begins to work its way outside through their decisions and actions. At first, their co-workers, friends, and family may not notice much of a change. They may still "talk" like they used to but then realize they shouldn't. They may visit old hangouts and places they used to party at but then feel checked in their hearts that they shouldn't return. Gradually, new Christ followers start changing their lives one decision at a time. Eventually, everyone who knew them before can clearly see that they're different now!

Reading the Bible is a powerful way to change from the inside out. We have a saying at our church: "You can't do better or be better until you know better." Daily reading of the Bible challenges our thinking and shows us a better way, a way that doesn't come naturally to us.

Listen as you read how Psalm 119:103-105 describes how desirable the Bible is to us:

How sweet your words taste to me; they are sweeter than honey. Your commandments give me understanding;

no wonder I hate every false way of life. Your word is a
lamp to guide my feet and a light for my path. (NLT)

Fix Your Glasses

Have you ever had a prescription for glasses or contacts that worked
great at one time but now just show the world as a blurry mess? There's
probably someone reading this sentence right now who's been putting
off going to the optometrist for a while, even though they know their
eyesight has changed.

What if I told you that we all wear prescriptions that influence the
way we see the world and what we think about it.

These unseen *lenses* of our mind alter the way we perceive and inter-
pret everything around us, including people, motives, actions, events,
and on, and on. These lenses were crafted for us by our family, school,
teachers, friends, church (or no church), TV, movies, books, and just
about anything around us as we grew up. Our lenses help us understand
and interact in this world. They can be very positive, neutral, or negative.
They can help us or hinder us.

The thing I find most interesting is that *most people don't even realize
that they're wearing any mental lenses!*

Paraphrasing William Shakespeare, "Such as we are made of, such
as we see." To make any kind of advancement in our life, we must recognize where we are in our current situation and then open ourselves
up to new ways of thinking.

A fun way of demonstrating how our invisible lenses impact our
thinking is take a look at this classic brain teaser. What do you see?

Depending on your perspective, you may see a beautiful young woman turning her face away, or you may see an old, hunched woman with a large nose and sad expression. Most people will instantly see one of the two possibilities and will then struggle to see the other, but believe it or not, both women are there!

When we are able to open our minds to the possibility of a new reality, we give ourselves the opportunity to experience life-changing growth.

Leo Tolstoy said, "Everyone thinks of changing the world, but no one thinks of changing himself."

Are You Listening?

One of the greatest ways I've experienced the power to change in my own life is for me to stop giving my opinion and to start asking others for their perspective. And let me tell you, there is a treasure trove of ancient wisdom in the Bible that is ready for you to listen to.

James 1:19 says, "You must all be quick to listen, slow to speak, and slow to get angry." (NLT) The "Jeff Paraphrased Version" is: Button up, listen up, and you'll grow up.

One Sunday after a service, a man came up to me and asked if could have a few minutes of my time. I politely nodded, and he replied that he wanted to talk to me about something I said during one of my messages the previous Sunday.

Now, having been a preacher for most of my life, the words, "I want to talk to you about something you said," can trigger a warning within me, since many people over the years have said these words before launching into a "critique" of something I preached. So in this case, even though I remained smiling on the outside, inside myself I said, "Oh boy, here we go."

"Stop asking *what you were thinking*," he said to me, echoing my own words from the stage from the previous Sunday, "and start asking *what are you thinking*."

I stared at him for a moment trying to figure out whether he was telling me that I needed to do this or that he didn't like what I'd said or that he actually liked what I'd said. I was lost.

The man then revealed that he worked for a car dealership owned by two brothers who were constantly fighting. Tensions had risen so much between them at work that they were threatening each other with dissolving the partnership and closing the dealership.

For whatever reason, the two brothers invited this man into a Monday morning meeting with them, and just as tensions between the two brothers threatened to flare up out of control again, this man bravely jumped from his seat and demanded, "Stop!"

With both brothers glaring at him in shock and with his job hanging on the line, the man counseled, "Hey, instead of you two sarcastically attacking each other with, 'What *were* you thinking?' how 'bout you ask each other, 'What *are* you thinking?'"

Dead silence filled the room. The two brothers exchanged glances. One resettled in his chair as the other cleared his throat. Then, after a long moment, one asked the other, "So...what *are* you thinking?"

It was a miracle! Instead of fighting, the two brothers carried on a civil conversation and actually listened to each other!

A wise person once said, "God gave us two ears and one mouth, so that we could listen twice as much as we speak."

Practice listening to bring positive change into your life.

Let Go of Pride

What is pride? Pride is when we think we've got everything figured out and we think we no longer need help or advice from anyone. A full-blown case of pride is when a person says to God, "I don't even need you!"

The Bible gives us many warnings of the destruction that pride can wreck in a person's life. Quite plainly, Proverbs 16:18 declares:

> Pride goes before destruction, and haughtiness before a fall. (NLT)

Pride can do great damage to relationships. Pride keeps score of when people have wronged us. Pride says, "I'm giving you this, *but* I want something in return." Pride says, "I don't need you."

We Can Be Blind to Our Pride

I went through a season in my life where pride flared up big time in my marriage. Interestingly, I was completely blind to it! If you'd asked me at the time if I were a prideful man, I'd have responded, "Who? Me? No way."

But then one day, my wife Rhonda and I were having an emotionally-charged disagreement. Tensions had been building between us for a while, and I thought the problem was all with her. I just didn't get where she was coming from. And then she revealed the root of her frustration with our situation.

"Jeff," she said with pain in her eyes, "I feel like you don't need me!"

Wow. Her words startled me. I felt like I had been stabbed in the heart, not by her but by my own realization that *I* had been hurting her— the very woman I love more than any other in the world!

I confess that I had a pride problem. From that moment, I began working to rid myself of this toxic idea that I don't need people. And I asked God to forgive me.

"Why ask God to forgive you?" you might ask.

Well, the answer is quite simple. James 4:6 says:

> God opposes the proud but gives grace to the humble. (NIV)

If pride was already separating me from my wife and others, it was slyly at work in the background of my life, separating me from God!

Chesnee Dorsey, a wise and long-term member of our church's staff, says it this way: "If you always have to be right, you'll end up alone." Notice the promises from God found in 1 Peter 5:6-7:

Humble yourselves, therefore, under God's mighty hand, that he may lift you up in due time. Casting all your care upon Him, for He cares for you. (NIV)

When we humble ourselves, God goes into action in regard to our situation and puts a "due time" on the delivery of the answer, just like a due date for a baby. After seeing my wife go through nine months of pregnancy twice, I have a better understanding of having to patiently wait for the due date.

Rhonda, on the other hand, was the one who *really* had to endure the uncomfortable waiting of pregnancy. The closer she got to the due date for each child, the more discomfort she had to endure, especially in the last days of both pregnancies. She would be going about her day like normal, and then suddenly, she'd pause and clutch her stomach as an early contraction would hit. Sometimes the pain lasted for fifteen minutes and would then pass. The closer she got to the due date, the stronger the contractions would be.

Finally, it was time, and the birthing process was the most painful of all. I have no idea how Rhonda endured so much pain, but in the end, she delivered two healthy children into our world!

I share these memories with you because you may still be waiting for answers to prayers, some of which you've prayed for a long time. If you're a Christ follower, I encourage you to humble yourself before God, ask him for an answer that will be best for you, and have faith that God will deliver on his promises.

The Old Wise Man

I'd like to retell to you a story that Zig Ziglar used many times to make people think.

High on a hilltop overlooking the picturesque city of Venice, there lived an old man who was a genius. Legend said that he could answer any question anyone brought to him. Two mischievous boys hatched a plan to fool the old man. They caught a small bird and headed up the long, steep path leading to the old man's home.

Upon finally arriving at the little house perched on top of the hill, the two boys saw the old wise man sitting on the front porch and walked up to him. Without any polite introductions, one of the boys thrust his two hands forward with the bird trapped inside. With a smirk at his friend, he challenged the old man. "Hey, old man, if you're so wise, is the bird inside my hands dead or alive?"

The wise man looked at the boys, already knowing the mischief in their hearts, and sat silently for a moment. Then, he leaned forward and replied, "My boy, if I answer that the bird is alive, you'll close your hands and crush the bird to death. If I reply that the bird is dead, you'll open your hands and let the bird fly away."

Shock appeared on the boy's face, followed by a flash of red from embarrassment. He glanced down at his hands and opened the little prison he had made. Instantly, the bird flew away into the cloudless sky.

The old man smiled and nodded his head at his visitors. "You've chosen well, my child. You understand now that you hold the power of life and death in your hands."

So take a moment and think of an answer to this question: What is one area of your life where you need to change?

If you feel comfortable saying it out loud, say it out loud. This is a very important moment because until you identify where you need to change and that you want to change, you won't be able to change.

Now ask God to help you take the actions you need to do to get your positive change started. He may guide you to an AA group, a church, a friend, a book, or a counselor. And by asking God for his help, you are humbling yourself before him. Remember James 4:6 from earlier?

> God opposes the proud but gives grace to the humble. (NIV)

If you have not already asked Jesus into your heart, now would be a great time to ask him. He's listening and ready to become your Savior, friend, and Lord if you will invite him in. Jesus is willing to save you from your sins and misdoings, and he is ready to give you a unique purpose for using your life to help others.

Ready to accept him? Pray the following prayer from your heart:

> Dear Lord Jesus, I know I'm a sinner, and I ask for your forgiveness. I believe that you died for my sins and rose from the dead. I trust you and will follow you as my Lord. Please help me to turn from my sins and to do your will. In Jesus' name I pray. Amen.

If you just prayed that prayer, I would love to hear from you! Send me an email to jeffdaws1@sccview.net, and I'll send you a free book on how to take your next steps as a Christ follower.

Making It Personal

1. What emotions come to you when you hear the word "change"?

2. Many great advancements came about because people were willing to see things differently. What areas in your life could benefit from a new way of thinking?

3. The negative form of pride can hurt and interfere with good relationships. Are you "keeping score" against someone? If so, give some thought as to why you're doing that. What would it take to change the way you think about that person?

4. The story of the two boys and a bird taught us that we have the power of life and death in our hands. What are some ways that you can use your hands to bring "life" to those around you?

5. An important step in positive personal change is to move from fixing the blame on someone to working on a fix for the problem. Be honest; how often do you catch yourself blaming others at home, work, or school? How could you approach problems at home, work, or school differently?

Chapter 2

A New Identity

*I*t was the first week of the new year, and I threw some workout clothes in my duffle bag and hopped in my car to drive to the gym I regularly visit. Finally arriving, I chuckled to myself as I saw the parking lot: It was packed! As I drove around looking for a parking space, I just kept smiling. You see, I knew a secret, but I was keeping it to myself.

After parking at a space way out in the lot, I walked to the entrance, flung open the door, and laughed to myself again as I scanned the room. There were people *everywhere!* The entire room was a frenzy of weightlifting, curling, pressing, jumping, cycling, jogging, squatting, and running! My feet instinctively started heading toward the exercise equipment station where I would normally start my morning routine, but I abruptly stopped, seeing that there was already a person at the station working out on it and a line of people waiting to use it after him.

In fact, everywhere I looked, every piece of equipment I normally used was taken!

After wading through the crowd and getting bumped and jostled, I made my way toward the back of the giant room, where a row of people—most of which looked like they were out of breath and about ready to collapse at any minute—were jogging on treadmills. There was one treadmill open, and it was the old one that nobody wanted to use. But with a smile, I hopped up onto its squeaky deck and punched a few scratched-up buttons. With a groan, the treadmill started, and I was finally on my way to getting in my morning workout.

So what was the secret that kept me smiling and laughing to myself while I endured this new crowd of people surrounding me? Simply this: I knew that they'd almost all be gone from the gym in a few weeks! Having seen this comical trend year after year, I knew that some of these people, who'd made New Year's resolutions to get into shape, wouldn't even be back the *next day!*

We all see things in our lives that we wish were different. It's become a national expectation to set New Year's resolutions to change the things in our lives we don't like. We set goals to lose weight, stop smoking, pay off credit cards, spend more time with our families, stop being so critical, start being a better spouse or parent or person.

But then...

Almost instantly we fall back into our old patterns of thinking and behavior. It's a real struggle of willpower, and quite frequently, our willpower just isn't strong enough. Yep, you read that correctly. I'm saying that our willpower alone is not enough.

I believe that to bring about real change in your life, you must start by asking yourself this question: Who do I want to become?

You may have never thought about this, but please understand that you can never be a different person from the person you see yourself as. Said another way, what you think about yourself and what you say about yourself define who you are.

The great news is that if you really want to change yourself, you can! But change will not come overnight. It will take work, time, and the changing of the way you think and talk about yourself.

And if you think I'm just making this up, remember that the Bible tells us over and over that becoming a different person, a *new person*, is part of being a Christ follower. Check out 2 Corinthians 5:17:

> When someone becomes a Christian, he becomes a brand-new person inside. He is not the same anymore. A new life has begun! (TLB)

Being a Christian means that I start seeing people more like the way Jesus sees them. "So how does Jesus see people?" you might ask. He sees through their exteriors and straight to their hearts.

The Person in the Mirror

Some years ago, I heard about a group of young people who were trying their best to share their faith in Jesus on the streets of Atlanta. Because everyone was in a hurry, it was almost impossible to enter into a conversation with anyone. And when someone finally stopped to talk, the noise of all the street traffic hindered any meaningful discussion.

Nevertheless, the young Christians refused to give up and persisted in witnessing to any and all pedestrians that passed by them, asking them, "Do you know Jesus as your personal Savior?" Despite people ignoring them, making fun of them, or even lashing out at them, they continued on their mission.

One day, a young man from the group of witnessing Christians saw a woman in nurse scrubs approaching and felt a tug on his heart. With a smile, he made eye contact with her and asked, "Do you know Jesus as your personal Savior?"

The woman stopped. With curiosity spreading across her face, she turned to the young man and simply replied, "No."

Excitement and anxiety raced through the young man. Stuttering his reply at first, he finally started quoting 2 Corinthians 5:17: "Therefore, if anyone is in Christ, he is a new creation; the old has gone, the new has come!"

The woman was intrigued. She stood still; her eyes fixed on his.

Not knowing what to say next, he immediately jumped to, "Would you like to receive this Jesus who can make you new?"

Barely heard over the roar of traffic, the woman replied, "Yes." She was tired of her old life and wanted to be different. She was ready to take a step of faith into something new.

The young man led her through the sinners' prayer, and right there, on a sidewalk in downtown Atlanta, she became a follower of Jesus.

Later that afternoon, she returned home. It had been a long day at work, and after she had flung her purse and satchel onto her bed, she beelined to her bathroom and took a long look at her face in the mirror. She sighed, not noticing any change in her appearance. All of the lines from worry and age as well as other imperfections were still there in the mirror. "Maybe it takes a while," she thought before turning and heading to the kitchen to make dinner.

That night, when she decided to retire to bed, she went back into the bathroom to look at the mirrored version of herself. Everything looked the same. "Maybe God didn't hear me," she reasoned, "or maybe it takes a while to go into effect."

Frowning, she hit the light switch and went to bed.

The next day, the woman jumped out of bed and raced across the room to check her mirror. Expecting to see some kind of change in her appearance, once again she was disappointed by the evidence staring back at her. With a long exhale, she continued her routine of getting ready for work and left her home.

On her way to work, she quietly prayed, "God, if you're real...if you can truly make me a new person, please show me some proof."

Upon arriving at work, she hurried through the parking lot to get inside. To her, everything looked the same—her co-workers' cars, random trash blown by the wind into the lot, some graffiti spray painted on a "No Parking" sign, the same drab office building in front of her. She raced up the steps to the office door and grabbed the door handle.

Suddenly, the woman froze.

A feeling like she had never felt before swept over her entire body. She paused, her hand literally unable to open the office door. For years, she had walked through this door as a matter of routine, never really giving much thought about it. But on this morning, she was overwhelmed with the sensation that something evil was waiting just on the other side of that door. Her hand trembled as a chill ran up her spine. It felt like *Death* itself was waiting for her just on the other side.

Something *had* changed within her, and it was telling her now that she needed turn around and *run* and to *never return!*

Without any further hesitation, the woman let go of the door handle, spun around, and fled the abortion clinic to never return.

To me, both of these people's intersecting stories are amazing and show how God can use us to spread the good news of Jesus Christ to others and that God really does listen to our prayers and is more than able to guide us by his Spirit in our lives. When we give our life to Jesus, he starts a life-long process of transforming us into a new person.

How we see ourselves has everything to do with who we become.

Jesus was constantly reminding people of who he was, and his actions reflected who he was. The question that we should all ask ourselves is, "Who do I want to become?"

Hoppin' Mad

When I was twenty-two years old, I was given an opportunity to serve in full time ministry as a student pastor in Toccoa, Georgia. The pastor of the church, Jerry Chitwood, took a chance on me. I hadn't had a lot of educational training and not much experience in ministry work. I was just a country boy who loved God and who had a burning desire to do God's work.

I thank God that Pastor Chitwood took me under his wing and became my mentor, because I was very, very green and rough around the edges. And not long after I started working as a student pastor, I needed his wisdom!

One evening, I was sitting with Rhonda watching TV in the little duplex apartment we were renting. The phone hanging on the kitchen wall rang, and I jumped up to answer it. Wondering who would be calling at this hour, I lifted the receiver from its cradle and said, "Hello?"

On the other end came a man's voice that I didn't recognize at first. His words were slurred, so I knew that he was drunk. And then my mind connected the voice with a face. He was the father of a teenage girl who had started attending our youth group.

Suddenly, the man began cursing and yelling all kinds of vile things at me. He was furious with me that his daughter had received Jesus into her life without his approval. The man didn't believe in God and felt that I had brainwashed his daughter.

At first, I tried to be respectful and not get pulled into his anger. But my heart was already racing, and when he snarled, "If I ever see you in town, I'm gonna open up a can of whoop *** on you!" I snapped.

While this was going on, Rhonda heard my voice getting tense and loud, so she came over to the phone to see what was happening. Instinctively, she knew I was about to make a bad decision and started waving her hands at me while mouthing, "No, Jeff, noooooo!"

But it was too late. I was hot as a fireplace poker and came right back with, "Fine! Where would you like to meet to see if you're man enough to do that?!"

CLICK

The caller hung up, and I slammed the phone back into its cradle. Rhonda gave me a look like, "What have you done?" But I was so hopped up on adrenaline, I didn't care. I was ready to fight!

Needless to say, neither Rhonda nor I slept well that night. I kept playing out fight scenarios in my head all night long, and every time I heard a sound, I jolted out of bed to see if he had come over to our apartment to finish the conversation.

But he never showed up.

———————

The next morning, I went to the church, thoughts of the conversation from the night before still racing through my mind. When I parked my car, I saw Pastor Chitwood sitting in his truck, waiting for me. We were headed to visit people in the hospital, and it had become our custom to have a "Monday meeting" in his truck as we rode along. And boy did I have something to tell him about!

As Pastor Chitwood drove, he asked me about how things were going, so I poked out my chest and proudly told him about how I had refused to back down to this guy's threats. I bragged about how I had accepted the man's challenge to fight and that I wasn't going to let some drunk atheist "run over me."

I just knew that Pastor Chitwood would be proud of me for not backing down when threatened. So I waited for his praise. And waited... and waited. The sound of road noise as we drove became very loud in my ears.

I glanced over at Pastor Chitwood and saw him smoothing his moustache with his index finger and thumb—a common tell that he was in deep thought.

The longer we sat in silence, the more I realized that he was not happy with what I had done.

Finally, Pastor Chitwood broke the silence by clearing his throat. I braced waiting to be ripped to shreds. I could tell that he was *very* unhappy with what I had done, and I readied for him to tell me that I needed to find a new place to work.

"Jeff," he began in a serious tone, "let me ask you a question."

"Okay," I sheepishly replied.

"Do you want to be a person of godly character?"

I swallowed hard. "Yes, sir. I do." I started sweating. I was in trouble!

"Jeff, do you think a man of godly character and of godly influence would have responded the way you did?"

I shook my head. My mistake was now crystal clear. "No, sir...I really messed up."

Pastor Chitwood got quiet again. It seemed like an eternity as I waited for his next words. I cringed expecting him to really tear me up, but when he continued, his response somehow corrected me *and* encouraged me.

"Son, remember this: You are an ambassador for Christ. And as such, you should act like Christ, even when other people act like the devil."

During this incident in my life, it's like I forgot who I was. I forgot my new identity in Christ and started acting like the old guy I used to be before I started following Jesus. After this incident, I began making different choices related to my new identity as a Christian. And it's a process.

Pastor Chitwood ended with this word of wisdom, that you can apply to your life as well: "When you know who you want to be, you will know what to do."

The Process

You may say, "Jeff, I want to change some things in my life, but I just don't know how to get started." Well, my friend, if that's you, let me help you get started with some simple steps to get you going on your journey to becoming a different person.

1.   Change how you identify yourself

In his book *Atomic Habits*, James Clear shares an example of two people who are trying to quit smoking. When the first person is offered a smoke, he responds, "No thanks, I'm trying to quit." This reply sounds good and valid at first. The person *is* truthfully trying to quit and had the willpower to temporarily turn down a free cigarette.

But now look at how the second person replies in the same scenario.

"Hey, wanna smoke?"

"No thanks, I'm not a smoker."

Wow! This is a very different response. The second person has now shifted identity from "I am a smoker who is trying to quit, but I really want to snatch that free cigarette out of your hand and light it up" to "I was a smoker, and I no longer have the desire for it."

You will never be different until you start seeing yourself differently.

So ask yourself, "Who do I want to become?" Answering this question gives you great reason to change.

Throughout my years as a pastor, I've had countless people privately share with me about the struggles they faced or still must confront because of poor decisions in their lives. Drug addiction, multiple sexual partners, and alcoholism are just some of the issues that people have lived in. But over and over, these same people say, "That wasn't me! I was miserable!"

I could hear their anguish. They wanted to be different; they wanted to start fresh and have a new life. And the great news is that through God and by seeing ourselves differently, we can be a different person and make wise choices.

Take a look at Proverbs 18:21:

Death and life are in the power of the tongue. (KJV)

According to the Bible, your own words about yourself can work for or against you! Here are some examples of negative declarations we make about ourselves and our abilities:

I'm just a screw up.
Everything I do turns out bad.
I'm a failure.
My life will never get better.

I'm a terrible student.
I'm always late.
I don't understand the Bible.
I can't live like a Christian should.
I'm a sickly person.
I'm not dependable.
I'm just stupid.
I ruin every relationship I get into.

So, what if—and just humor me here if you're skeptical—we told ourselves the opposite?

I learn from my mistakes.
I do great work.
I'm successful.
My life is getting better every day.
I'm a great student.
I'm punctual.
God helps me understand the Bible.
I am a Christian.
I'm healthy.
I'm dependable.
I'm intelligent.
I build strong and lasting relationships.

I don't know about you, but when I read the first list, I feel pretty down in the dumps about myself and about life in general! But when I read the second list, I feel energized, excited, and ready to take on life daily!

I encourage you to start seeing yourself and talking about yourself differently every day. And you can do this by writing down on a piece of paper or notecard a simple list of positive declarations about yourself. Put this list somewhere you'll see it every day, and when you do, read them out loud.

Think about it: By hearing you confess your list of positive qualities every day, you'll start changing the way you think about yourself, and you'll start to become the person you've written about!

What's in a Name?

I find it very interesting that in Genesis 17:15-16, God changed the name of Sarai to Sarah to demonstrate that Sarah was now a new person. Take a look:

> Then God added, "Regarding Sarai your wife—her name is no longer 'Sarai' but 'Sarah' ('Princess'). And I will bless her and give you a son from her! Yes, I will bless her richly, and make her the mother of nations!" (TLB)

From that point forward, people literally called her a different name. God did the same with Abram, changing his name to "Abraham." But why?

The name change meant that they were new people, very different from before this special blessing from God. Sarai went from simply being Abram's wife to the "mother of nations." And that's how she started living.

Abram went from being a nomad with flocks of sheep to being the father of nations. And the Bible records in its genealogies that millions and millions of people came from Abraham and Sarah's lineage. In truth, you may be a distant genetic descendant of Abraham and Sarah, a living proof that God keeps his word!

An example of this name change also occurred in the New Testament in John 1:42, when Jesus said to Simon, one of his disciples, "You are Simon, John's son—but you shall be called Peter, the rock!" (TLB)

Prior to following Jesus, Simon was a very rough fisherman, given over to vices and other unsavory behavior. But Jesus saw the potential in Simon. And when Jesus invited Simon to follow him, Simon left his fishing boat and his way of living and became one of the disciples.

Even further, when Jesus changed Simon's name to Peter, "Peter" is the name that we are all familiar with, and it was this Peter who went on to become one of the most important and influential Christians in the early church. He was literally like a stone, strong and unmoving like granite, in his devotion to Jesus and the church after Christ's resurrection.

The way you see yourself changes everything.

You Won't Amount to Anything

When Victor Serebriakoff was a child in London, he found school very frustrating. He would raise his hand in class to answer as many questions as he could, but this just invited constant bullying from the other kids in class, who would make fun of him and throw things at him as they chased him home after school. At age fifteen, he had a teacher who continually shamed him in class, calling him a "dunce" and telling him that he'd never finish school. And so, Victor did just that. He dropped out of school and went to work at a lumber company.

For the next seventeen years, he wandered from job to job, unhappy with his life and unable to figure out how to change for the better. He was a "dunce" after all; what can they accomplish in life?

Years passed, and World War II exploded across Europe and the world. England was in deep need for able-bodied men to become soldiers, so Victor enlisted. During the entrance process, he was given a standardized Army intelligence test to evaluate his I.Q.

And when he finally was told the result, his mouth dropped! He had an I.Q. of at least 161—an exceptionally high result!

From that moment on, Victor changed the way he thought about himself and literally changed as a person. As opposed to being scattered with details, he trained himself to organize his thinking. After the war, he returned to the timber business and patented a machine for grading timber, even becoming the manager of a sawmill.

Victor then joined Mensa, an organization for people with high I.Q.s, eventually becoming its chairman. He even wrote several books on intelligence, personality, and puzzles. And all of this from a man who had been classified as a "dunce" who would never amount to anything!

My question to you is: Who are you allowing to define who you are? Consider Proverbs 23:7:

For as he thinks in his heart, so is he. (NKJV)

When you know who you want to be, then you will know what to do.

2.   Behave like the person you want to become

Your identity rises out of the way you think about yourself and out of the many actions you perform each day. For instance, by folding your clothes after they've dried and putting them away in your bureau, wardrobe, or closet, you're exhibiting the traits of someone who is organized. On the flip side, if you just leave your clothes in the dryer and pull out a wrinkled shirt each day, you're showing signs of someone who puts things off. And if you just leave your wet clothes in the washing machine for a week, that's pretty disgusting! You're definitely not demonstrating the qualities of a CEO.

So if you're interested in changing who you are and don't know where to start, begin with your daily and weekly routines. Instead of thinking about things like exercising, reading the Bible, praying, doing the dishes, cleaning the bathroom, vacuuming, mowing the lawn, doing the laundry, and so on, like chores (which we learned to try to avoid in childhood), think of them as *opportunities* to become a *new* you! Think of your daily life as a way to start practicing what you're learning in this book.

And this applies to work as well. (Now buckle your seatbelt because I'm going to make this real.) Instead of waiting to work on projects at the last minute, avoiding certain co-workers because you're afraid they might ask you to do something, showing up late every other day, sneaking long breaks so you can watch Netflix or play games on your phone, gossiping about co-workers, undermining your supervisor, hanging out on social media while you're supposed to be updating a spreadsheet, pretending to talk to customers while you're really talking to friends or family, and on, and on...

...INSTEAD, what if you acted at work like you were an investor in the business? What if you acted like a partial owner who only gets paid if the business grows and prospers? Would that change how you act at work?

I can tell you one thing for certain: If you change who you are at work by changing how you act at work, you're going to start enjoying work more and the people around you are going to notice the change. And if you stay committed to being different, your chances for a raise, promotion, or transfer to an area you really like will greatly increase!

In his book *Atomic Habits*, James Clear states, "Every action you take is a vote for the type of person you wish to become."

I read of a woman who lost 100 pounds simply by asking herself "What would a healthy person do?" Every time she was tempted to eat something deep fried or super sweet, she'd ask herself that same question. When she was tired and really just wanted to sit on the couch, watching TV and snacking on junk food, she'd ask herself, "What would a healthy person do?" And she'd get up and head over to her treadmill and start exercising.

So who do you want to become?

3. Write out and say daily declarations about who you are

If at this point you're saying, "Yes, Jeff, I do want to become someone different, but it seems like every time I try, I end up back where I started," I understand what you mean. You're not alone. The Apostle Paul himself, despite being one of the most influential Christians to have ever lived and who wrote many books of the New Testament, had days where he felt like he went backward.

In Romans 7:21-25, Paul confesses:

> "When I want to do good, evil is right there with me." (NIV)

Paul goes on to thank God for the mercy and grace he received through Jesus, and this goes for us as well. As a follower of Jesus, his Holy Spirit dwells within us and encourages us to make the right choices.

The Apostle Paul even goes further in Romans 8:35-37 saying that hardship, persecution, hunger, poverty, danger and even death cannot separate us from the love of Christ. That through the power of God, we have been made more than conquerors in Christ!

Let that sink into your mind and heart. If you're a Christian, you have the power to be more than a conqueror! You're not a victim of your circumstances; you can be victorious through your godly identity.

Make That List

In this chapter, I've challenged you to think of *who* you'd like to be. Hopefully you've got a set of positive qualities and traits that you'd like to become a part of your daily life.

Now, it's time to start getting the ball rolling on your own personal change. If you haven't already done so, I want you to write down those qualities you desire to become and make them into a positive declaration about yourself.

Here's what my daily declaration looks like:

> I am a follower of Jesus, and I bring honor to God.
> I am a husband who is passionate about his wife.
> I am a father who loves and communicates with his children.
> I am a person who speaks life.
> I am a pastor who loves his people.
> I am a leader of leaders.
> I am a person who fears less.

I am generous.

I am a person who gives people an opportunity for a better life.

I am a man who uses words with restraint.

Every morning, I read through my list of declarations out loud. By hearing my own positive statements about myself and about who I want to be, I find myself moving toward these statements with my decisions throughout my day.

I promise you that if you add this simple one-minute action to your daily routine, you will start seeing positive change in your life. Start today and give it a try for twenty-one days and watch how your thinking about yourself changes, your actions toward yourself and others change, and your journey toward a better *you* begins.

What do you have to lose? You've got so much to gain!

Making It Personal

1. The beginning of a new year is the most popular time for people to make changes in their lives. Do you make New Year's resolutions? If so, what is your track record for keeping them?

2. To help change what we are like as a person, we must ask ourselves who we want to become like. Who do you want to become? What qualities would you like to have?

3. The way we see ourselves shows up many times in the way we talk about ourselves. Your words can work for or against you. What do you need to stop saying about yourself? What do you need to start saying about yourself?

4. Looking at the statement, "When you know who you want to become, then you'll know what to do," what actions do you need to start taking in your life to make your vision of yourself a reality?

5. CHALLENGE: Saying daily declarations about specific qualities you want to develop in your life is an important way to help
   you make these changes a reality. Get a 3x5 card and write down
   5 positive declarations about yourself. When you are finished
   with your list, say them out loud and continue saying them out
   loud every morning for the next 21 days. In 21 days, come back
   to this page and evaluate any changes you have observed in
   yourself and your life. You can also adjust these 5 declarations
   to better fit who you want to become.

Chapter 3

Let It Go

*I*n 2013, Disney released an animated movie called *Frozen*, and since then, hearing the three words "Let It Go" instantly launches most people into hearing or even singing the lead song of that movie, whether they like it or not.

Putting the song aside, letting go of things that have hurt you in the past can be great advice. And it sounds easy. You've probably had people ask you before, "Why can't you just let that go?"

Fear, pain, anger, and other negative emotions that grew out of bad experiences have a way of weighing us down and holding us back. When you were born, you most likely only had two fears: the fear of loud noises and the fear of falling. As time has moved forward, your brain has identified a host of new dangers and scenarios where you could be physically and *emotionally* injured.

And our desire to avoid fear sells!

Just think about all of the products for sale whose chief selling point is that they can help protect you and your family. Alarm companies run commercials with a family (played by actors, of course) being woken up in the night to the sound of smashed glass and the blaring of an alarm.

Thank goodness they had XYZ Alarm Company to magically make the robbers run away! A car company shows their latest model vehicle veering out of its lane. Suddenly a warning dings and flashes on the dashboard. Oops! Better get back in my lane. And have you seen the newest children's car seats? Wow, they're like straight out of NASCAR.

A few years ago, Rhonda and I got to take home a five-month-old tyke named Drew. He's the son of our Family Pastor Chesnee Dorsey, and Rhonda and I have been friends with their family for decades and have become like godparents to Drew. Before leaving church on this day, Drew's father Danny installed the car seat in the back of my car and buckled in Drew.

We waved goodbye to Danny and Chesnee and drove home. It was a hot day, so we were ready to go into action like a NASCAR pit crew. Rhonda jumped out and grabbed Drew's bag, toys, and the food we'd picked up on the way home. I hopped out, opened the back door, and pulled on the strap to release Drew from the car seat.

But...nothing happened.

I found another strap and pulled it. Nothing. Beads of sweat appeared and started running down my forehead. What was the deal with this car seat?!

Rhonda called from inside the house, "Hey, Jeff, you comin'?"

"In a sec!" I replied, my face all scrunched up as I tried to figure out the mystery of the car seat. Now, baby Drew was starting to sweat from the heat, and he looked up at me with big eyes and made a face like "Get me out of here!"

Finally, Rhonda came back outside to see what was happening. By then, I was very agitated and could tell that, in any second, Drew was going to start crying and that our ideal time together was going to be ruined.

While I continued struggling with the child seat from Hades, Rhonda called Danny for help. She pushed the phone to my ear, and he calmly walked me through the steps to release Drew from his car seat. In a flash, the child was free from his car seat prison, and I scooped him up and took him inside to the A.C.

Security alarms, safety features on vehicles, car seats for children, and the countless other products marketed to us to protect ourselves and families are great; I'm not criticizing them. I use them!

I'm merely drawing attention to the truth that as humans, we are naturally *fearful*. And, if we're not aware of how our own fears can impact our decisions and beliefs, we can allow fear to absolutely ruin our relationships and lives.

1. Relax your fear guard

We think of fear as a negative emotion. It's definitely not fun. You can probably think back to your childhood and remember times that you were scared. Maybe you saw shadows in your bedroom as monsters or thought something was living under your bed or in your closet. I'm not even going to bring up the whole thing about clowns.

You may remember being afraid of learning to ride a bike or learning to skate or learning to swim. And then came the bike accident or the falls in front of people or getting caught in a current. These were definitely not fun. But for most of you, your younger self pushed through and achieved the ability to do these things. You learned to quiet your fear and live with it.

In a positive light, God put protective instincts within us to help us survive. The problem comes when we allow fear to run our lives.

That Left Turn

I was recently reminded of what it feels like to be overwhelmed by fear.

One early morning, I was leaving the gym after my workout, headed back to the church. I came up to an intersection on a four-lane highway and needed to turn left, but there was a "No Left Turn" sign. I glanced down the road at how far I'd have to drive before I could make a legal left turn.

I shook my head. "It's still early in the morning," I thought, "and there's practically no traffic. No one will notice."

So I made the left turn, and no sooner had I done so, blue lights flashed on behind me. With a sinking feeling in my stomach, I pulled over on the side of the road. It had been several years since I'd been pulled over by the police. Looking in the rearview mirror at the police cruiser behind me, I tried to calm myself by reasoning, "It was a traffic sign infraction. It'll probably just be a small fine, and I'll be on my way."

The next thing I know, I catch sight out of my side mirror of a police officer slowly moving down the side of my car toward me. I don't know why, but that sight sent my heart racing. I lowered my window and put my hands on the steering wheel.

When the officer got to my window, he asked me in a serious tone, "Where are you headed in such a hurry, sir?"

I swallowed and replied, "To work, officer." (Somehow, saying that I was on my way to church just didn't fit.)

"Did you notice the "No Left Turn" sign at the intersection?" he asked.

I nodded slowly. "Yes, sir, I did see the sign."

"So why did you make the turn?"

I could feel myself wanting to sink into the floorboard of my car.

"Well, officer, I was...in a hurry."

The officer gave me a look like "Really? You don't say."

I felt God tapping me on the shoulder to confess to my wrongdoing, and so I did. "Officer, it was wrong of me to make that turn. It's my fault, and I'm very sorry I did it. Thank you for all you do to keep our community safe. I know you have to write me a ticket, so here's my driver's license." I handed my license through the window and waited.

The police officer received my license and stood there for a moment, studying me. I could feel the tension inside me going down. He studied my license and said, "Mr. Daws, I'll be right back."

And with that, he walked back to his cruiser to write down my information.

As I waited for his return, I realized the severity of my simple left turn. In addition to not heeding the sign, I had potentially risked my life and that of other people by launching my car into an area of low visibility. I learned later that many accidents have taken place in that spot, and that's why there's a "No Left Turn" sign there.

I can tell you this: I won't be making a left turn at that intersection again! I will drive all the way down to the next turning lane and retrace my route before risking my life and someone else's.

I tell this story because fear can make us defensive. Any time someone does something that reminds us of a past hurt or fear, we tend to put up our defensive walls or run by avoiding the person completely. "Fight or flight" is a real thing.

Antidote to Fear

One of the greatest antidotes to fear is prayer. Philippians 4:6-7 gives us this winning formula to lower fear:

Do not be anxious about anything, but in everything, by prayer and petition, with thanksgiving, present your requests to God. And the peace of God, which transcends all understanding, will guard your hearts and your minds in Christ Jesus. (NIV)

The Apostle Paul is saying here that when our prayers go up, our fear goes down. We've adapted this concept into several sayings at SCC, such as, "When my worship goes up, my worry comes down." We say, "When my praise goes up, my panic comes down." And one of my favorites, "A prayer-filled mind is a peace-filled life."

Take a moment now to take a deep breath...release it...and drop your shoulders...thanking God for that breath you just received and released.

Do it again and enjoy it. Any time you're feeling overwhelmed use this simple technique to reset yourself. You can also incorporate Scripture as you relax. Consider 1 John 4:18:

There is no fear in love. But perfect love drives out fear. (NIV)

Either fear is going to drive out love or love is going to drive out fear. My question for you is which are you allowing to grow within yourself? Fear is automatic. Love is not automatic; it is learned. I heard one of our staff pastors Chris Woodson say that "loving is learning," and I believe that this is very true.

2. Recognize the fear, feel it, and then release it

I find it interesting that whenever feelings like anger, hurt, insecurity, jealousy, or embarrassment arise within us, they want us to hold on to them. We can't stop these feelings from coming, but we can choose whether to hold them or let them go.

Jeff, Stand and Read

When I was in elementary school, I had a problem reading. Years later, I'd find out that I have attention-deficit disorder and mild dyslexia, but at that time, I had no clue.

In class, teachers would ask me to read out loud, and I hated it! I'd stumble and stammer over words, while the other kids in class smoothly read through their passages. My classmates made fun of me, laughed at me, and said that I was "dumb."

Because of these embarrassing moments, I was terrified to read in front of people. I'd do anything in school to protect myself from further embarrassment, even if it meant failing a class. I even had to repeat third grade.

My fear of reading out loud led to a complete fear of reading period! I hated books, hated reading, and hated writing. So when I became a Christian in high school and my mentor told me that I needed to read the Bible daily, I groaned in anguish. I literally associated pain and terror with anything related to reading.

And then, God ironically called me to preach his Word!

I had visions of myself, standing in front of church, with hundreds of eyes on me, just waiting for me to read a Bible verse and mess up so that they could laugh at me. I just knew that if I accepted God's call, I would be the laughingstock of the church world.

Nevertheless, my mentor, Randy Brooks, encouraged me to start reading on my own at home. He told me, "Jeff, leaders are readers," and he gave me the book *Improving Your Serve* by Charles Swindoll. It was the first book I'd ever read from cover to cover, and I remember feeling so proud of myself for accomplishing something I didn't think I could do!

As I accepted God's call on my life and began working in the ministry, I'd love to say that God snapped his fingers and instantly healed whatever was causing my reading issues. But he didn't. Instead, it has been a slow, intentional process on my part to read the Bible, along with other books, daily. I also began writing a little bit every day some years ago, and that has led me to writing and publishing four books now.

Wow! From the kid who failed third grade to writing books! I'm telling you, once you start taking on your fears one by one and challenging yourself, you'll see some amazing results over time if you stay with it.

One of the first books I read to help me change the way I saw myself was Zig Ziglar's *See You at the Top*. I started realizing that much of my problem with reading was fear. I had to put to silence the old memories of kids making fun of me so that I could develop into the leader that God called me to be.

I had to "silence the rooster." If you're thinking, "What does *that* mean?" let me tell you a story from the life of Booker T. Washington.

Silence the Rooster

As a child, being a slave on a plantation, Booker T. Washington was awakened every morning by the crowing of a rooster. And he hated it.

Every morning the rooster would start making its loud racket before the sun even came up. Eventually, the rooster came to symbolize the imprisoned life, the long days, and the backbreaking labor of a slave.

But then, Abraham Lincoln delivered the Emancipation Proclamation and pronounced freedom for all slaves. Word of this landmark decision spread quickly, and the next morning, as Booker was waking up, he heard the rooster making all kinds of ruckus. But when he opened his eyes, he couldn't believe what he saw: His mother was chasing the rooster around the barnyard with an ax! The Washington family fried and ate their alarm clock for lunch, effectively silencing their reminder of slavery.

What "rooster" in your life, past or present, do you need to silence?

What is it that comes to mind that holds you back whenever you start to step forward to be different?

Voices, heckling me from my past, imprisoned me in fear for a long, long time. I finally chose to challenge them and let go of my past so that I could go forward. I had to stop taking myself so seriously when I mispronounced words and just have a chuckle at myself.

When I finally released fear, guess what, it finally let go of me. And I want to encourage you that it can be the same for you. Whatever fears hold you back, there is hope when you recognize them, acknowledge the feelings associated with them, and release them.

Your brightest and greatest days are ahead of you!

Making It Personal

1. One of the biggest battles we face in changing ourselves for the better is what we hold on to. What is something in your life that you're still holding on to, maybe even from long ago? How could you let it go?

2. Fear and anxiety can deter us from letting go of things from the past that we know we need to release. Read Philippians 4:6-7. According to these verses, what is our spiritual weapon against fear and anxiety?

3. The next time you find yourself fearful, angry, or anxious, what if instead of a usual response you turned to prayer first? What would it take for you to make this possible in your life?

4. Read 1 John 4:18. Notice that fear can suppress love and that love can drive away fear. Looking at your average day, which would you say is more active inside of you: fear or love?

5. Fear is a natural part of being human, but that does not mean that we have to be victims to fear. Preparing for the future, what could be a new plan of action for you when you start to feel fear building up inside of you?

6. In the story of Booker T. Washington, his mother silenced the rooster. What "rooster" in your life do you need to silence?

Chapter 4

Discover Yourself

When I was fifteen years old, Rhonda and I started being friends, and once I got my driver's license, we started dating. After graduating from high school, we married, and you might think after dating all those years that we'd know each other perfectly well. You might believe that we never discovered any surprises about each other.

Well, surprise! That's just not true. My life proves that you really don't know someone until you live with them, 24/7, 365 days a year, through the seasons, through sickness, for several years.

And once Rhonda and I were married, we discovered that we were very different. Surprise, surprise! She was quiet; I was very loud. Her family environment was very calm; they rarely raised their voices. It seemed like they were always looking out for each other.

When it came to my family while I was growing up, it seemed like we were constantly in some turmoil, with drama and kids fighting, since there were always a bunch of kids in the house. We raised our voices to get attention, to fight over who controlled the toys or the TV, and to vent our frustrations at each other. Now, my family members loved each other, but there were plenty of times we sure didn't like each other.

So after Rhonda and I married and we started getting to know each other's personality and quirks, we discovered that we were almost complete opposites! I've found through life that opposites attract in relationships and then attack.

Nevertheless, Rhonda and I have been married for over thirty years.

You might be wondering how we've stayed together all these years and even grown closer as we've gotten older. To begin with, we both are committed to Jesus Christ. We both have an ongoing, daily relationship with him, and we both seek to serve him with our lives. Jesus has been our anchoring rock throughout all of the storms that our marriage has gone through, and he will continue to be our rock as we go through the rest of the seasons of our lives.

The second key that has kept our relationship strong is that both of us had to learn to change. I truly believe that we can't be better or do better until we know better. So, we had to intentionally learn about ourselves and each other.

John Maxwell says it this way: "Learning means to change, and if you haven't changed, you haven't learned."

So what about you? Who are you? What do you like about yourself? What do you wish were different about yourself?

If you're interested in learning more about the path you can take to develop yourself into a better *you*, read on.

Do You Know Him?

When people ask me to help them get started in becoming a better person, I always start with asking them if they have given their life to Jesus. I know this may seem cliché to some of you (a pastor asking people if they know Jesus), but I promise you that if you go through life and never know Jesus as your personal Savior and never live for him, then all the change you'd like to make in your life is a complete waste of time. This life is just the beginning of our existence, and my friend, trust me, you want to be on the side that gets to enjoy the splendor of heaven for all eternity and not the other place!

2 Corinthians 5:17 plainly says:

> Anyone who belongs to Christ is a new person. The past
> is forgotten, and everything is new. (CEV)

When I became a Christian as a teenager, it was so weird to me for a while. Praying was new to me, and I really didn't know how to do it. I sat in church actually listening to the preacher as opposed to sitting on the back row throwing spitballs at people.

Not cussing was new to me and a struggle for a while as my mouth caught up to my changing thinking. Trying to live a clean life was new too. And I suddenly had a desire to learn, which was new. I started transforming from a person who didn't really care about life to someone who had a completely new look on life's opportunities.

If you haven't accepted Jesus as your Lord and Savior, I would encourage you with everything within me to do so. I want to make sure that you, too, have the opportunity to experience a new life here as well as life in the next.

The Big Four

The next step in my personal change came from John Maxwell. I was listening to one of his many leadership lessons, and he shared about a book that was a game changer for him when he was younger and struggling to become a better person. So I bought *How to Understand Others by Understanding Yourself* by Florence Littauer, and it opened my eyes to the four basic personality types that all people can be categorized in.

Here's a condensed summary of the four personality types she describes in great detail in her book.

The Powerful Choleric

As a strength, these people tend to be strong leaders. They are action-oriented and prefer things done sooner rather than later. Weaknesses of the choleric personality are that they can easily offend others in their rush to get things done and can come off as being arrogant and aggressive.

The Popular Sanguine

The strength of sanguines is their fun-loving nature. They love socializing, chatting, and telling stories. Weaknesses of the sanguine personality are that they tend to over-promise and under-deliver and feel that they have to be the center of attention.

The Peaceful Phlegmatic

Phlegmatics are laid back and foster a peaceful environment. They tend to be excellent negotiators since they want everyone to be happy. As a weakness, this personality type does not like to make decisions, preferring the status quo, which may frustrate the other personality types. They also tend to not like conflict and will go to great lengths to avoid it.

The Perfect Melancholy

People with a melancholy personality tend to be great at analyzing and evaluating all kinds of information and scenarios. They tend to catch small details that the other personalities miss and can be very creative. As a weakness, melancholies tend to fall victim to "analysis-paralysis," where they get stuck in analyzing all the possible outcomes of a scenario. This can irk the other personalities who are waiting for a simple solution.

If you're curious about discovering more about your personality and those of others, I highly recommend that you read her book. It greatly impacted the way I thought about myself and Rhonda. You see, for years I thought something was wrong with Rhonda. She didn't see the world the way I saw it, and she didn't interact with people the way I did.

But after reading Florence Littauer's book, I experienced an "Ah ha" moment. Rhonda and I have very different personalities. I'm Choleric, and she's Phlegmatic—at two extremes of the personality chart. I want to confront issues of disagreement by arguing my case like a lawyer. She wants to preserve the peace by remaining calm and letting go of things that she doesn't feel are extremely important.

You might be asking right now, "What good does it do me to know what personality I have and what personality my spouse or friend or family member or co-worker has?"

Knowing how the four personality types think and how they react in situations can be a tremendous help to building strong relationships with everyone.

For instance, I know that I can wear my feelings on my sleeves. So I am much more aware of this now, and when I start to notice that I'm going down that road of just letting my raw emotions spew out all over my peace-loving wife, I choose to change and pull back the way I'm expressing what I'm feeling inside.

For Rhonda, she knows that her personality would much rather not have a difficult conversation, especially if it might disrupt the peace. But after reading Littauer's book, she's also aware that having difficult conversations is the only way to get to the root of misunderstandings and disagreements. So, trust me, she's learned to change and speak up when she needs to!

Having a knowledge of the four personality types also helps Christians be able to reach out to everyone in the name of Jesus. Many times, we can be guilty of just writing people off as rude, insensitive, lazy, glory-seeking, judgmental, and so on, thinking that they're singling us out for ill-treatment. I encourage you the next time that you run into this type of situation to ask yourself, "Is it just my personality conflicting with their personality?"

If it is a personality conflict, then there's hope that you can work through it to build a meaningful relationship with them.

What's Your Love Language?

In 1992, Gary Chapman published a book entitled *The Five Love Languages,* and it became a tremendous success. It's still in publication today, helping couples build stronger relationships.

I remember the first time I heard about this book. I was preaching a marriage series on Sundays at my church. After one service, Diane Cardin, a talented and creative woman who'd been attending our church for years, came up to me and said, "Hey Jeff, there's this book that would tie in great with what you're preaching about!"

And she wouldn't let me forget about it! She kept asking me if I'd gotten it yet, so I finally bought it and started reading it.

Dr. Gary Chapman is an associate pastor over families and counseling. As he practiced counseling, he was amazed and troubled by a pattern he saw over and over again. Good people, who were married and who genuinely seemed to love each other, were on a sad highway to divorce.

The common thread that Dr. Chapman kept observing was that these couples had no idea how to effectively communicate their love to their spouse. As I said before, the irony about relationships is that opposites attract, and Dr. Chapman discovered that this is true about the way that we like to express and receive expressions of love and appreciation.

By an overwhelming majority, most spouses have opposite ways of sharing love.

You Want *What*?!

Now, you already know that Rhonda and I are very different. Here's how our different love languages complicated our relationship and then later strengthened our marriage.

When I was growing up, my father did all of the exterior upkeep of the house, and my stepmother did all of the inside work. My father also worked two jobs, so this was the behavior modeled to me as "normal."

After getting married, I mowed the lawn and took care of the house exterior, but I would not help Rhonda with chores like cooking, dishes, vacuuming, etc. At the time, I believed that those things were her responsibility and that she needed to live up to "her responsibilities." I also worked a second job, like my father, which meant that I had little free time at home.

Well, eventually Rhonda had had enough, and she confronted me. "I married you to be with you," she sternly reminded me.

I countered with, "I'll quit the second job, and when you have house work, I'll do outside work like washing the cars."

She shook her head. "You're not getting what I'm saying. I want to spend time with you. How about we both do the house chores together and we both work in the yard and wash the cars."

In hindsight, my sweet wife Rhonda was screaming to spend time with me because her primary love language is Quality Time. But this didn't make sense to me until we read the Love Languages book. And I wasn't the only one in the dark. Rhonda didn't get my love language either.

We'd be riding in the car, and I'd slide my hand over onto the armrest between the two seats and start reaching for her hand to hold. But suddenly, her hand would withdraw. After this happened repeatedly, I began to think that she was mad at me for something I had done or that she was just teasing me. I began to think that she was repulsed by my touch. To me it seemed like she was trying to avoid me touching her at all costs.

And then I'd get angry. Whenever we arrived at our destination, I'd throw the car in park, jerk the key out of the ignition, rip off my seatbelt, fling open the door, jump out of the car, and slam the door!

In looking back, poor Rhonda had no clue what was going on inside of me. She'd ask me, "Jeff, what's wrong?" I would just give her a cutting look that said, "You know what's wrong." But she truly didn't know.

The knowledge that Rhonda was missing before reading the Love Languages book is that my primary love language is Touch. This is why I kept trying to hold her hand. I was trying to give her love the way I like it, but it was doing nothing for her, and then I felt rejected.

Boy, I look back at our lives before we learned each other's primary love language and just shake my head at how *hard* we were trying to show love to each other but kept missing what the other wanted. She'd get up at 4:30 in the morning to show her love for me by making me breakfast before I headed off to work. The food was great, but I could've just as easily stopped at a fast-food place on the way in. I'd give her a hug in public to show my affection for her, and after three seconds, she'd tap me on the shoulder and whisper, "That's enough." And when I tried to give her a kiss in front of people, she'd shy away.

We were caught in a maddening cycle that would repeat over and over until the tension would build up to a boiling point, and we'd fight. And then the cycle would start all over again...until we learned each other's love language.

You can't be better or do better until you know better.

Do you know your love language? Do you know the love language of your spouse? Here are the five love languages and a short description of each. To get the full benefit of this relationship breakthrough, you need to read *The Five Love Languages*. You can use these concepts in all kinds of relationships, and if you're married, I encourage you to read this book with your spouse.

1. **Words of Affirmation**

   These people love encouragement, appreciation, and to be heard.

   These people don't like criticism or failing to recognize their efforts.

2. **Physical Touch**

   These people love simple physical touch in all its forms.

These people don't like physical neglect.

3. **Receiving Gifts**

These people love thoughtful gifts. Small gifts matter a lot to them.

These people don't like it when special occasions are forgotten.

4. **Quality Time**

These people love uninterrupted time together and special moments together.

These people don't like distractions and lack of conversation.

5. **Acts of Service**

These people love to help out and enjoy working together.

These people don't like being marginalized and forgotten.

Self-discovery is critical for all of us, and learning plus putting our learning into practice is a sweet recipe for success in relationships. Growing ourselves and our bonds with others is a life-long process. It's a journey that I pray you will take. And I can assure you that as we get better, our lives get better!

Making It Personal

1. Read 2 Corinthians 5:17. What were some of the changes you noticed in yourself after you accepted Jesus as your Savior?

2. Looking at the four personality types mentioned in the chapter, which personality are you like most of the time? What about the people who are closest to you?

3. If you are currently experiencing conflict with someone, where do you think their personality fits into the big four? Could your difficulties with this person result from a conflict of

personalities? If so, what could you do in light of their personality traits that could help with the relationship?

4. Take a moment to glance back over the five love languages discussed in this chapter. What is your top love language? (Most people will have a primary and secondary.) Have people been trying to express love to you in ways that do not fit who you are? If so, how could you gently let them know how you would prefer to be shown love?

5. If you are married, what is the love language of your spouse? If you don't know, have them read that section of this chapter and let you know their top two. How could this knowledge help the future of your marriage relationship?

6. CHALLENGE: The five love languages are at work in all relationships that have a loving bond. Give some thought to what the main love language of three people close to you is. These could be children, parents, siblings, and close friends.

Chapter 5

Pursue the Right *Who*

*H*ave you ever been sitting at a railroad crossing, watching all the rail cars blur by in front of you? I confess, I'm rather an impatient person, so when I see the railroad crossing arms lower and see the red flashing lights, I'm like, "Great! How long am I going to have to sit here?"

Well, if you find yourself sitting at a railroad crossing, let me give you something to look forward to that will give you a clue as to how long you're going to be sitting there. If the train starts with one engine, rejoice! You probably won't be there very long. Two engines mean you'll be there a little bit, and if there are five engines, I hope you brought your lunch with you!

But on one occasion, when I was sitting in my car, stuck in a line of traffic, waiting for this long train to end, I made an observation that can be applied to our lives. The rail cars were all connected, and one by one, they followed the engine.

At first glance, you may think, "What's so profound about that, Jeff? That's how trains work."

The important observation is that *your connections determine your direction*. So for a moment, I want you to picture the "who" in your life—the people you are surrounded by every week. See their faces in your mind. Who are these people? Family, friends, co-workers, acquaintances, people you spend time with. Who are they?

Whether you realize it or not, the people you've pictured have an influence on your life, some positive, some not so positive. And what direction are they pointing with their lives? As the old saying goes, *"More is caught than taught."*

So I'll ask you this question: Are the people you choose to hang around going in a direction with their lives that you want to journey toward yourself? If they're not, I believe that you need to give some serious thought to changing who you hang out with.

Now, let me be clear; I'm *not* talking about family here. God placed you in your family to shine the light of his love to them. And family is... family. I'm talking about the *optional* people you surround yourself with. It's your choice, and I can tell you that many people reading these words right now are connected with people who are taking them in a different direction than they really want to go.

We can't upgrade our family, but we can "upgrade" many of our other relationships if we choose to.

Um, Where's Jesus?

In the Bible, Luke chapter two describes a fascinating moment in Jesus' early life. His parents had taken him to a feast in Jerusalem called Passover. It was a celebration of how God had miraculously preserved the lives of the Jews in Egypt and then delivered them from there.

For Jesus' family, the walk to Jerusalem took many days, but they journeyed with a host of people from their town for company and protection. After enjoying the feast, Jesus' family packed up their belongings and headed back home. But after a day of travel, Mary and Joseph couldn't find Jesus. In a panic, they headed back to Jerusalem, hoping that he was still there. For three days, they endlessly searched the crowded streets of the city, frantically looking for their son. Luke 2:46-49 records what happened next:

> After three days, they found him in the temple courts, sitting among the teachers, listening to them and asking them questions...When his parents saw him, they were astonished. His mother said to him, "Son, why have you treated us like this? Your father and I have been anxiously searching for you." "Why were you searching for me?" he asked. "Didn't you know I had to be in my Father's house?" (NIV)

I like this story because it shows some of the human side of Jesus. I chuckle when I think about him ditching his family to hang out with the priests and religious people for a few more days. And when his parents asked him why he had done this, Jesus simply replied that he wanted to be in his Father's house, the Temple.

I don't know if Jesus was punished, but the Bible does say that he was obedient to his parents when they left Jerusalem the second time.

The point I'd like to focus on from this scene is that even at an early age, Jesus, who is our example in all things, was connecting with people who he believed would be helpful to him. For three days, he sat, listened to, and conversed with some of the most brilliant, religious minds of the Jewish faith during that time. He went to the "experts" as such to learn from them.

Jesus also felt an overwhelming desire to connect with God the Father, the giver of knowledge and wisdom, and the creator of all.

So here's some practical steps I recommend if you'd like to upgrade your relationships.

1. Place yourself around the right people

Just like Jesus sought out people who were very good at what they did, seek out friendships with people who are very good at what interests you. It's up to you to go to them; don't wait for them to come to you—that's not going to happen. You have to strike up the conversations and go to where they are. Even if your first few attempts don't work out, take joy in knowing that you are actively choosing to change your life and take hope in knowing that eventually the right relationships will come along!

One of the greatest mistakes I made in my life was not seeking out people who were better than me at something. Instead of learning from these people along my life's walk, I felt insecure around them and stayed away. When I think of all the opportunities I missed along the way, I groan deeply within. But then I remind myself that I still have years left to learn, and I challenge myself to not give in to insecurity and fear.

My turning point at becoming a better pastor and leader was when I established a connection with Scott Sheppard, pastor of Cornerstone Church in Athens, Georgia. I had seen him many times at gatherings, but other than cordial greetings, I just stayed to myself.

But then I intentionally started hanging around him at meetings. This man had a way of thinking that I lacked, and I wanted to change. I started connecting with him outside of these meetings, and we became good friends. I greatly admired his abilities to lead and grow a church.

So I started asking him all kinds of questions. I don't know if he ever got tired of me asking him, "How did you...?" and "How would you...?" But Scott is a very gracious man of God, and he always had an answer or nugget of wisdom for me.

And when we attended meetings, he started introducing me to lots of knowledgeable people. He'd open up with, "This is Jeff Daws! (Handshake) You need to get to know him!" I'd stand there shaking the person's hand, thinking to myself, "Who is Scott talking about?!"

I cannot overemphasize the importance of pursuing a connection with people who are better at something than you!

2. Listen to them

As I say often at church, "We can't be better or do better until we know better," and the best way to "know better" is to listen to people. This is something that I haven't been very good at in my life. I start off listening to people, and then I switch into Mr. Fix It Mode and give out advice about how people can fix their problems. But I'm choosing to change this, and I'm learning how to listen better and *doing it.*

Jesus himself in the Temple sat listening to people. The power of change comes when we listen to those around us. To grow is to change, and to change is to listen. Don't be like the fool in Proverbs 18:2:

> Fools do not want to understand anything. They only
> want to tell others what they think. (NCV)

We can get stuck in life by always giving out our opinions and not seeking out new knowledge. By just recycling what's in our minds, we're not renewing our minds. Recycling what our parents said or our friends said doesn't really help us change or grow.

Instead of trying to tell everyone what you think, start asking people what they think. Listening is learning.

VHS Gold

Rhonda and I were very young when we were married and had little knowledge of how to handle finances, marriage, and parenting. For the longest time, we just practiced what we had seen our parents do. But eventually, we came to a point where we were stuck and needed help. However, I confess that I was too prideful at the time to seek outside help. I didn't want people to think that Rhonda and I were having problems. But the problems were real.

One day, Rhonda had found some old VHS tapes at the church by a family counselor and marriage expert named Gary Smalley, and she said, "Hey Jeff, look what I found!"

I took one look at the dusty tapes and thought, "Looks like you found junk." Of course, that's *not* what I said out loud.

Rhonda was set on watching these tapes together, so I reluctantly agreed. But inside my heart, I was extremely skeptical that some guy could teach me anything useful. You see, I had learned growing up that a wife served her husband by taking care of everything at home as well as his needs. I believed that a man's responsibility was to work, bring home a paycheck, defend the home and mow the lawn, but that's about it. Well, maybe I barbecued every now and then. But still, I believed that I was doing everything right, which meant that obviously Rhonda was doing something wrong.

Or so I thought.

In the first lesson, I rolled my eyes a few times, but then Gary Smalley taught that a husband should honor his wife like a Stradivarius violin—a rare and valuable treasure, to be treated with tenderness and respect.

Wow, that concept really jarred me! I'd told Rhonda that I loved her many times, but I hadn't extended the level of public and private respect to her that I needed to.

Watching these lessons were a major turning point in our marriage. And we started learning from other experts as well. For financial learning, we turned to Larry Burkett and Dave Ramsey—both of whom revolutionized our beliefs and behavior with money.

In James 1:19, the Bible encourages us to learn by listening:

> Understand this, my dear brothers and sisters: You must all be quick to listen, slow to speak, and slow to get angry. (NLT)

I mean, just look in a mirror. God gave you two ears and one mouth. It's a strong message that he wanted us to listen twice as much as we speak. But be sure to surround yourself with the right people to listen to.

I tell you: *You can't be better or do better until you know better.*

3. Ask the people around you questions

For years, I've been reading the books and listening to the messages of one of our world's greatest leadership experts, John Maxwell. He literally has open invitations to speak at countless conventions, conferences, and other gatherings all around the world. Even though he doesn't know me, this man's brilliance in leadership has tremendously influenced my thinking, leading, and teaching.

And from him I learned that *asking questions* is key to supercharging the change you desire in your life.

E I E I O

Pastor Benny Tate of Rock Springs Church is another person who has poured wisdom into my life. For years, I'd hear him on the radio at night as I drove. He's a powerful speaker, and God has blessed him with the knowledge of how to build a church with over six thousand in attendance on weekends in the middle of nowhere, Milner, Georgia! He jokes all the time that their church's zip code is *E I E I O*, like the kid's song "Old McDonald."

Suddenly one day, I thought, "I need to meet this extraordinary man and learn from him." But then I got a bit scared and backed away from this crazy notion. You see, Pastor Tate is constantly on the move. In addition to lead-pastoring a massive church, he speaks at countless venues all throughout the week. One day he's at a church, hours away; then he's at the Capitol building in downtown Atlanta; then he's speaking at a business luncheon; then he's in Washington D.C. opening Congress with prayer. It seems like he's everywhere, which makes his time valuable.

I ditched the idea to contact him, but then God prodded me with, "Call his church."

"Okay, here I go," I thought, and I dialed the number of the church. I could feel my hands getting sweaty. "Maybe I should just hang up," I thought.

Then a friendly voice answered with, "It's a great day at Rock Springs Church; how can I help you?"

I explained who I was and said that I'd like to schedule a meeting with Pastor Tate for thirty minutes and that I would be happy to compensate him for his time.

The woman on the line politely replied, "I'm sure he'd like to meet you, but he won't want you to pay." And she connected me with Pastor Tate's personal assistant Julie to work out the details. But then Julie said the fateful words I've heard so many times: "I'll look at his calendar and get back with you." Usually this means, "I don't want to hurt your feelings, but he's too busy to meet you."

So I returned my desk phone to its receiver and consoled myself with, "Well, at least I tried."

Two days later, I got a call from Julie out of the blue. She said, "Pastor Benny is available on Friday at 2pm."

Before she could say anything else, I blurted out, "I'll be there!"

And that's what I did!

I showed up early and got to meet both the people I had spoken with on the phone. And when it came time for my thirty-minute meeting, Pastor Benny greeted me with a big, warm smile and boomed, "How in the world are you doing, Jeff?"

It all seemed like I was dreaming. Thankfully, I had written down the questions I wanted to ask him ahead of time and sent them to him so he could be prepared. And when Pastor Benny launched into answering them, I scribbled as fast as I could in a notepad, trying my best to keep up with him. I felt like there was smoke coming off the paper I was writing so fast!

The meeting flew by, and as I got up to shake his hand and thank him, he smiled and promised, "Jeff, as long as you have questions, I have the time."

And that was the beginning of my mentoring relationship with this amazing, caring, generous, and phenomenal leader!

So now I ask you, who would you like to learn from? Who could you contact to set up a thirty-minute meeting to ask some questions you'd like answered? My friend, there is so much beneficial knowledge and wisdom out there for the asking if you'd just take the time to do what most people *don't* do.

Let the following words of Jesus from Matthew 7:7-8 inspire you to step out of your comfort zone and step into a better you:

> Ask and it will be given to you; seek and you will find; knock and the door will be opened to you. For everyone who asks receives; the one who seeks finds; and to the one who knocks, the door will be opened. (NIV)

Making It Personal

1. Just like the engine on a train pulls its cars in the direction its going, your connections determine your life's direction. Take a moment to think about the people around you throughout the week. Who is having a positive pull on your life? Who is having a negative pull on your life?

2. Think about a time in your life when a friend pulled you in the wrong direction. What happened? What did you do to get yourself going in the right direction?

3. Take a moment to think about some of your favorite interests. (These could be related to work, pastimes, talents, skills, and so on.) Now thinking of your top favorites, do you know someone who is better at them than you?

4. In reference to the previous question, if you know someone who is better at something than you, how could you reach out to them to learn from them?

5. Read James 1:19. Asking questions is key to supercharging positive change in your life. Who in your life could you contact and set up a meeting to ask some questions you'd like answered?

6. Read Matthew 7:7-8. How could these verses be an inspiration to you as you seek out knowledge, wisdom, and training in your life?

Chapter 6

Watch Your Mouth

When you were growing up, did a parent or teacher tell you to watch your mouth? Mine sure did! For me, it was like my mouth was always getting me in trouble. My mom used to warn me, "Jeff, your jaybird mouth is gonna get your mockingbird backside in a whole lot of trouble!"

Solomon, one of the wisest people in history, taught in Proverbs 21:23 (CEV), "Watching what you say can save you a lot of trouble." And I give a huge "amen" to that.

Our words are powerful. Joe Dobbins, a friend of mine, said, "Your words are the steering wheel of your life," and I've never forgotten it. At our church we say, "If you don't like what you're seeing, watch what you're saying!"

However, we tend to get into ruts of thinking and ruts of talking. If we really want to set a new course for our life, we need to climb out of these ruts and begin to speak life into our life.

But how do we do this?

1. Stop the negative self-talk

What you *think* determines what you *believe*, and what you *believe* determines how you *behave*. In my book *Your Opportunity for a Better Life*, I discuss the problem of negative self-talk by defining it as an *ANT* problem: Automatic Negative Thoughts.

Thoughts like "I always mess up" and "This is just the way I am" and "I'm a failure" are examples of automatic negative thoughts. These ideas are like a parade of ants marching into ears. Well, my friend, to grow into a better person you'll have to deal with this ANT infestation, and here's how to get started.

We Believe What We Say to Ourselves

When you realize you have an automatic negative thought go through your head, immediately replace it with something positive. If you thought, "I always mess up," you could rebuttal with, "I made a mistake, but I'm improving my life every day." Redirect, "This is just the way I am," with, "I'm making better choices every day." Challenge, "I'm a failure," with, "I'm learning to get better every day."

Say It Out Loud

A few years back, Rhonda and I were shocked when we found out that two of our good friends in the ministry both had severe crises in their marriages within a few months of the other.

Rhonda and I looked at each other and thought, "Could this happen to us?"

Choosing to be proactive, we decided to go to counseling to work on making our marriage stronger. The counselor asked Rhonda what she needed from me to make her feel loved, and Rhonda responded with, "Spend more time with me and do things around the house and in the yard together."

Now here's the key action that the counselor had me do. After Rhonda responded to the questions, the counselor had *me* repeat what Rhonda had just said. At first, this seemed a little silly to me. In my mind, I was like, "Duh, I know what she said; she just said it!"

But as both Rhonda and I started repeating what each of us said in our own words, it was like something clicked inside our minds, and we both *understood* what the other person said and *believed* it. Saying something out loud has the amazing ability to plant an idea deep into our mind. Say it enough times, and you'll believe it.

There is power in what we say to ourselves about ourselves!

The reformer Martin Luther said, "You cannot keep birds from flying over your head, but you can keep them from building a nest in your hair."

Do a *Word* Substitution

You can also stop ANTs by replacing negative thoughts with God's Word—the Bible. Romans 12:2 says:

> Do not conform any longer to the pattern of this world, but be transformed by the renewing of your mind. (NIV)

And Jesus told us in Matthew 22:37-39 to:

Love the Lord your God with all your heart, with all
your soul, and with all your mind. This is the greatest
and the most important commandment. The second
most important commandment is like it: Love your
neighbor as you love yourself. (GNT)

Notice in these verses that we are to love our neighbor as we love
ourselves. I know that some of you reading this page right now don't
like or love yourself. In fact, you may hate yourself. But there is hope
in Jesus of forgiveness of the wrongdoings of your past and hope to
have a healthy view of how valuable you are to God.

We can't really show love to others until we accept God's love for
us. When I say that we should have "love for ourselves," I'm not talking
about selfish, self-centeredness. I'm talking about having an appreciation for ourselves as treasures in God's eyes, treasures that he loved so
much that he came into our world to die for our sins so that we could
reconnect with him.

By pondering and accepting the love God has for us, we can then
share this love with our neighbors—our family, friends, next-door
neighbors, co-workers, strangers, and even enemies!

If you have a problem accepting God's love, try this: Stand in front
of a mirror and say out loud, "God loves me, and I love me." This may
seem a bit strange to some, but if you're having trouble with negative
thoughts about yourself, substitute those downers by confessing that
God loves you and that because of that, you can love yourself.

Think on Good Things

The Apostle Paul, who originally persecuted Christians but then became a follower of Jesus, encouraged us in Philippians 4:8 to:

> Think about things that are pure and lovely, and dwell
> on the fine, good things in others. Think about all you
> can praise God for and be glad about. (TLB)

If you're having an ANT problem, I challenge you to read this simple but powerful verse in the morning before you start your work or school day for 21 days. When ANTs pop up as the day goes along, switch over to thinking about something pure, something lovely, something good, something that you can praise God for! This one practice alone could transform your life!

2. Speak words of life to others

I read about a survey that asked Americans what they most longed to hear. And you know what the two top answers were? "I love you," and, "I forgive you."

Wow, think about that. The next time you're walking down a street, eating in a restaurant, and shopping at a store, most of the people there are dying to hear that someone loves them or that they are forgiven for something wrong they did. To me that's amazing, because as Christ followers, we have the good news that God loves them, desires to have a relationship with them, and would love to forgive their sins!

I have to add here that the third most longed for thing to hear is "Dinner's ready!" And who could argue with that!

Power in the Tongue

This may seem odd at first, but Proverbs 18:21 (NIV) declares, "The tongue has the power of life and death." Literally, the words we speak to ourselves and others bring life or death, especially into our relationships.

Consider Proverbs 17:27:

> A person of knowledge uses words with restraint, and
> a person of understanding is even-tempered. (NIV)

The strongest people I know are the meekest people I know. When I say this, sometimes people give me a confused look. It's a good possibility that this statement confuses people because they think *meekness* is *weakness*.

What images come to mind when I say the "strongest people?"

A weightlifter? Superman? Wonder Woman? The Rock, Dwayne Johnson? People able to pull semi-trucks with their teeth?

What if I told you that some of the strongest people are actually physically weak?

That might've lost some of you, but here's the powerful truth in the previous verse: Meekness is power under control. For instance, horses are extremely powerful animals. They can run at speeds faster than any human can run with an endurance that far out does what we can do. Yet, a horse can be trained to the point that a child can ride it! That is an amazing picture of power under control.

Controlling our tongue requires meekness, power under control.

Bank Robbery Gone Bad

In his book *Never Split the Difference,* former FBI negotiator Chris Voss describes an unforgettable moment in his life.

He had been called in to assist in a hostage negotiation at a bank. The robbers had taken customers and employees as hostages. By the time that Chris arrived, people inside the bank had already been shot, the police had surrounded the building with snipers on rooftops, and the leader of the bank robbers was threatening more violence unless his demands were met. The outlook was bleak. It looked like more blood was going to be spilled.

Chris knew from his experience that the first thing he needed to do was to calm down the leader to deescalate the overwhelming tension. So when Chris finally got the leader on the phone, he spoke to him in a low, soft, relaxing tone, what he calls his "DJ voice."

After several hours of back and forth on the phone, Chris' calm technique built rapport with the leader of the bank robbers. When Chris quietly said, "I know you didn't want to do this," the leader agreed and surrendered!

This true event demonstrates that the way we speak to other people matters. When we change the way we speak to others, it can change everything!

When it comes to family, I say, "To change your home, change your tone." Jesus refers to this power of change in our words in Matthew 15:11:

> It's not what goes into your mouth that defiles you;
> you are defiled by the words that come out of your
> mouth. (NLT)

Defile means to make unclean or impure or offensive.

For example, if I worked out for two hours at the gym and sweated like crazy and then put my dirty, dripping-wet clothes in my gym bag after changing in the locker room and then zipped up the bag and left those nasty clothes sitting in that bag for a week, the next time I opened that bag, I'd be knocked over by the stink of mildew and B.O. Worse, I would've defiled my gym bag! I wouldn't dare put any clean clothes in it until I had washed it or maybe thrown it out and bought a new one.

Let's face it; our words can really stink! The way we talk to people—especially our own family members—can be rotten. But we can choose to change the way we talk to people, and that can really change our lives.

Remember, "If I don't like what I'm seeing, I must watch what I'm saying."

Open Mouth, Insert Foot

Before I became the pastor of SCC, I worked for a man who had just moved to the South from the North. Now we all know that there are regional differences all across America, and this can influence how people talk and think. And in every part of the U.S., you'll find people who are nice and some who are not so nice.

But for whatever reason, this man didn't really like Southerners. He told me one time, "Jeff, you know what the problem with Southerners is?"

Having lived my whole life in the South, I was a bit agitated by his remark but also curious what his observation was. "No, what is it?" I replied.

He pushed his shoulders back and said, "You Southerners always beat around the bush about things instead of just coming out and saying what's on your mind."

I didn't respond, but I did file away his comment in my mind.

Sunday came, and he preached his sermon with gusto. However, his message didn't really impact me. (Hey, preachers have bad days, too.)

And then Monday arrived, and as we ran into each other in the hallway, he stopped me and asked, "Jeff, what did you think about my sermon Sunday?"

I, remembering what this man had told me just a few days before, boldly stated, "Well, sir, your sermon wasn't very good."

Oh boy! Even as the words were falling out of my mouth, I knew that I had said the wrong thing, and this man—who claimed that he valued people who spoke their mind—turned red as a beet and proceeded to blast me for being disrespectful to him.

I wish I had a photo of my face at that moment! I bet that I looked confused, baffled, and probably a bit scared!

Our words matter, and they have a way of coming back to us in one way or another. Jesus said in Luke 6:38:

> Give, and it will be given to you...For with the measure
> you use, it will be measured to you. (NIV)

Most of the time, we read this verse in a positive light. If we help people, help will come back to us. And this is true and backed up by other verses in the Bible. But remember it works both ways. If we use our words to hurt people or mistreat people, that will come back on us as well.

So, are you using your mouth to spread blessings or cursing? You get to choose.

3. Speak words of faith in God

If we're going to get out of the ruts I talked about earlier, we can do so by speaking about our faith in God. Some of the roots of anxiety and depression find their roots in being overly self-focused.

During World War II, Corrie ten Boom and her family went from being simple Dutch watchmakers to radical criminals, risking their lives to break the law. And do you know what their crime was? Hiding Jews from the Nazi regime that had overtaken Amsterdam.

Eventually, the ten Boom safehouse was discovered by the Gestapo, and the family was thrown into the Ravensbruck Concentration Camp. The living conditions were horrific, with far too many people being crammed into cell blocks with no amenities like heat. The food was dreadful, if they were fed. Fleas infested their foul straw mattresses, and every day, they lived with the dread that their name would be called to be sent to the gas chamber.

But in this vile, heart-breaking darkness, Corrie discovered an earth-shaking truth. She said:

> *"If you look at the world, you'll be distressed. If you look within, you'll be depressed. But if you look at God, you'll be at rest."*

One day, Corrie suddenly felt like God spoke to her and promised her that he'd deliver her and her sister Betsie. But sadly, Betsie died in the camp. Nevertheless, Corrie held strong to the promise she received from God and spoke about her hope in God with the other prisoners in her cell block.

And miraculously, one day, Corrie was released from the hellish death camp. It was discovered later after the war that Corrie had been "accidentally" released by a clerical error just days before she would've been sent to the death chambers of Ravensbruck.

But Corrie knew that God had saved her, and for the rest of her life, she spoke wherever she could about the depths of horror that she experienced and about the love of God that was *even deeper*.

Speak words of faith in God to yourself and to others.

Could You Fix That Blind?

A few years ago, my father's house needed some repairs, and Dad didn't have the money on hand to pay for the work. So, he went to a bank and borrowed the money to cover the expense of the repairs.

He was approved for the loan; however, its terms were not good. I don't think my father quite understood that he had just signed a line of credit on his house that had to be paid off in six months. If he couldn't pay off the loan, he'd have to at least pay a lump sum of interest to then extend the loan pay off further into the future.

Now, my father is a praying man, and during one of his prayers after the loan, he said that God told him, "This one is on me."

After a few months, no help to pay the loan showed up. The due date loomed closer, but my dad maintained his faith in God providing a way to pay off this loan. He professed to our family, "I know what God said to me, and I believe it. God is going to show up and take care of this bill."

The weekend before the loan was due, my father and stepmother visited their local Waffle House to enjoy some time together with a freshly made waffle. But where they were sitting, the sun was beaming into Dad's eyes. So they asked their server to adjust the blinds.

BOOOOOM!!

The entire set of metal blinds crashed down on my father, gashing his head. The server apologized over and over as she grabbed a towel and applied it to his head.

"It's nothing; it's nothing," my dad said as he waved off all the attention that he was now getting from everybody in the restaurant.

The gash was deep enough to require stitches to get it to stop bleeding, so my stepmother took him to the hospital to be patched up.

After this event, several people advised my father to get a lawyer to sue Waffle House for negligence. But my father shook off these ideas. "It was an accident," he said. "It's not like she ripped that thing off the wall and dropped it on my head on purpose."

Then a phone call came for my dad. On the other end was a representative from Waffle House, who apologized for what had happened and sympathized with what my father and stepmother had gone through. The representative ended the call by saying that Waffle House would be sending them something to express their hope that my father would remain a customer of Waffle House.

So my dad hung up the phone, looking forward to receiving a gift certificate to Waffle House in the mail.

When the "something" finally arrived in the mail, my father almost collapsed when he opened the envelope and saw a check for the exact amount of money that he needed to pay off the line of credit! And talk about timing! The arrival of the check was just in time to settle the deposit in his checking account so that he could pay off the loan a day early! As Dad always says, "God is an on-time God!"

To this day, my father has a scar on his forehead, but every time he looks in the mirror, it reminds him of the financial miracle God worked out for him.

Now, please hear me. I'm *not* advocating taking out loans and expecting God to pay them off for you. I'm always encouraging people to take Dave Ramsey's Financial Peace course to learn how to manage money so that they can avoid being held prisoner in a debt trap forever. So don't run out to a car lot or bank and take out a big ole loan thinking, "Well, Jeff says God's gonna pay off my loan." That is not what I'm saying here at all.

What I *am* saying is that there was a need and God provided. Furthermore, my dad held to a promise that God gave him, and Dad persistently confessed his faith in God's faithfulness in fulfilling his promises to others.

I think of Psalm 19:14, which says:

> May the words of my mouth and the meditation of my
> heart be pleasing in your sight, O LORD, my Rock
> and my Redeemer. (NIV)

Here is God's cure for worry and fear! Here is one of the secrets to supercharging your faith and boosting positive change in your life! By using your mouth to speak words pleasing to God and by choosing to linger on thoughts that please God, you will find God to be your Rock and your Redeemer.

Like Jesus said in Mark 11:23:

Truly I tell you, if anyone says to this mountain, 'Go, throw yourself into the sea,' and does not doubt in their heart but believes that what they say will happen, it will be done for them. (NIV)

Use your tongue, mouth, and words as a trinity of blessing to breathe life into your own life and that of others. Counter those inner negative thoughts you have about yourself with positive declarations of who you are becoming. Grow your faith in God by speaking of the good things that God has done in your life and the lives of others, and I promise you that your life will change in so many good ways over time that you won't be able to even count all the blessings that you'll receive along this amazing journey.

Will you start today by substituting something negative you were going to say with something positive instead?

Making It Personal

1. What are some examples of negative self-talk that you have heard in your mind recently?

2. Referencing your answers to the previous question, how could you turn those negative thoughts into helpful, positive declarations?

3. Read Philippians 4:8. How might reading this verse every morning change your outlook on your day?

4. Try this: Find someone to practice your listening skills on and repeat back to them in your words what they said to you. This is a great communication technique to learn and practice because it helps to eliminate misunderstanding in conversation.

5. Read Matthew 15:11. Think back over this week at how you have spoken to people. How would you describe the tone of the words you used? If you were on the other side of these conversations, how would the tone and word choice impact you?

6. What does the statement, "To change your home, change your tone," mean to you?

7. Read Psalm 19:14. What is something good that God has done for you that you can focus on tomorrow throughout the day?

Chapter 7

Release It

*A*few years ago, Rhonda and I were sitting on the couch in our living room, flipping through the TV channels, looking for something to watch. We'd established a nighttime routine of watching a show together from 9pm to 10pm. We liked *Everybody Loves Raymond*, but we'd already seen all of the episodes.

So on this particular evening, Rhonda snatched the remote control and flipped it to HGTV, and a show called *Fixer Upper* was playing. I really wanted to watch something else, but as we spent an hour with Chip and Joanna Gaines as they remodeled houses, I've got to confess, I started enjoying the show.

As we watched more and more episodes, something started happening inside Rhonda. She's always been really good at interior decorating, and I noticed that she was suddenly spending hours sifting through stacks of paint color samples, flooring samples, and upholstery swashes. (Frankly, that kind of stuff bores me out of my mind, but Rhonda, on the other hand, looks like a kid in a candy store!)

And then it happened!

One evening, we were watching *Fixer Upper*, and Rhonda turned to me and matter-of-factly said, "Jeff, we can do that." I kind of just chuckled at the idea, but those words didn't happen just once; they became a regular part of us watching the show.

We'd watch Chip and Joanna demo a kitchen with a sledgehammer, and I'd hear, "We can do that!" We'd see them put up new cabinets in a kitchen, and I'd hear, "Jeff, you know we can do that!" Chip and Joanna would put in a "coffered ceiling featuring three-dimensional grooved wood to create an air of interest and *drama!*" (What a mouthful.) And, yep, Rhonda would declare, "We can do that."

Before I knew it, I too was convinced that we could renovate an old house. I mean, how hard could it be? We'd already seen two experts on TV show us how to do it many, many times. So together, we launched out on our mission to find a suitable house to fix up in our area—and we found one and bought it!

Next in the process was selling our other house, which shockingly happened much faster than we expected. So now, Rhonda and I had an old house to renovate and nowhere to sleep. Somehow, this was starting to feel quite different from the TV show. But we soldiered onward, parking a small travel trailer in the driveway of our new house!

Demo Day—the day on the TV show where Chip and Joanna excitedly charge into a fixer upper and smash out the walls and old cabinets—came, and Rhonda and I charged into our fixer upper with sledgehammers. I have to admit, it was quite fun to smash into the sheetrock of the ugly walls...at first.

What they don't show you on TV is that it's very tiring to keep swinging a sledgehammer for hours. Exhausted after our first day of demo work, we both stepped back, looked at each other, and evaluated our progress. We weren't even close to where we envisioned ourselves to be. We both sighed and went to our trailer to rest. Reality hit us much harder than we were expecting.

But Rhonda and I refused to quit. We encouraged each other when the other person was down, and we turned to God for help all the time, and I mean ALL the time! And it was amazing that every time we hit a problem, he provided an answer.

And then, after many months of backbreaking work, we moved into our new home. After living in a cramped trailer, our fixer upper felt like a palace! Both Rhonda and I looked at what we had accomplished, and we marveled at how God had partnered with us to make so many pieces come together when needed to complete the project. Praise God!

This experience taught me more than ever that I need the help of others; I can't live life alone. There's no way I would've been able to do all that needed to be done to fix up that house without the tireless efforts of my wife and of the contractors we hired to help with things that were beyond what Rhonda and I could do.

To bring about positive change in our lives, we need to learn to trust God and learn to work better with people.

So at this point, you might raise your hand and say, "Hold up, Jeff. You don't know what *this person* did to me; you don't know how they hurt me," or, "I can't trust my family." You might say, "I'm super discouraged right now, Jeff, and I don't even see the point in trying to make myself better," or you might add, "I've tried to change but failed so many times. It just seems pointless to try again."

If you've thought any of these statements, I hear you! You're not alone. My life has had many moments when I was miserable with my situation, surroundings, and relationships. But I'm here to tell you that it's possible to make yourself better, and when you get better, your life will get better.

I'm going to show you some of the important steps I've taken along my journey to move forward, and I'm going to share with you the passages in the Bible which have helped me get better. I pray that they will help you, too!

1. Release your family from past hurts

When I think of mixed-up family drama and relational pain in the Bible, my mind goes to David, the young shepherd boy who took down Goliath with his slingshot and later became the second king of Israel. He also wrote a good portion of the book of Psalms and was described as a man after God's own heart.

However, from the start, David was looked down upon by his older brothers. Being the youngest brother, he tended the sheep and goats, a pretty smelly and boring job, not glamorous like being a warrior in the army. So when a bearded prophet randomly showed up one day at their home, the brothers and their father Jesse were confused by what happened.

As recorded in 1 Samuel 16:11-13, God had sent the prophet Samuel to anoint the next king of Israel. Samuel started with the oldest brother, but God told him that he wasn't the one to be king. As Samuel went down the line of brothers, he got to the last one, and God didn't select any of them!

> Then Samuel asked, "Are these all the sons you have?"
> "There is still the youngest," Jesse replied. "But he's out in the fields watching the sheep and goats." "Send for him at once," Samuel said. (NLT)

When David arrived, sweaty and filthy from being out in the fields, God immediately told Samuel the prophet, "This is the one." And in the great tradition, Samuel anointed David with olive oil and blessed him.

Now imagine how the brothers felt watching this spectacle. God had clearly rejected all of them and chose the youngest to be the next king. I guarantee you that whatever sibling rivalry existed before the prophet showed up, the tension became worse for young David.

Eliab and Goliath?

Fast forward a little in David's life, and one day, his father sent him to take food to his brothers who were in Israel's army. As David walked along, divvying up food to his brothers, his oldest brother Eliab caught sight of him and flipped out on David. Check out how Eliab greets his youngest brother in 1 Samuel 17:28:

> "What are you doing here, anyway? Who's taking care of that little flock of sheep out in the desert? You spoiled brat! You came here just to watch the fighting, didn't you?" (CEV)

You can just feel the "love" in those words. I'm sure that Eliab felt overlooked by God and by his family. In ancient times, the firstborn son should have received the most respect of all a family's children. The greatest part of any inheritance would also go to the firstborn son in most families of the time.

However, in Eliab's case, it seemed the only thing he would be collecting was bitterness toward God and David. But it didn't have to be that way.

Most likely you know the epic story of David and Goliath, which took place shortly after David's visit to his brothers on the frontline. With a stone, a slingshot, and God's blessing, David took down the towering, armored giant Goliath while his brothers looked on in fear, horror, and envy.

Now here's something you may have never considered: Eliab had the same opportunity as David to fight Goliath. He *could* have given it a go! He might have died; he might have been blessed by God for stepping out against the challenger of Israel's army as David did. Growing up, we might have even been told the story of "Eliab and Goliath."

But instead, Eliab sat off to the side, stewing in fear, bitterness, and unforgiveness. And unless you're really good at Bible trivia, you've probably never even heard of him!

Ouch!

Family disappointments and hurts can be some of the deepest wounds we experience in life. But having experienced many myself, I can tell you that we've only got three options in how to deal with them.

We can replay the pain over and over in our mind and become bitter victims—which traps us in a cage of hate and leaves us a powerless victim forever. We can ignore what happened and pretend like all that went down never happened—which is a lie because what happened actually happened and our minds know this. Or we can forgive the people who hurt us and release ourselves from the trap of wanting to get revenge—which is the best advice I could give myself and you.

Option 3 is the only route I know of that leads to true healing in a person's heart and empowers them to move forward with their life. And don't get me wrong; it's not easy. It's much easier for our human nature to pretend like nothing happened or to stew in self-pity and vengeful anger.

Don't let something that was a temporary pain fester into a permanent pain in your life!

If you truly want to bring a weight-lifting freedom to your life from old family wounds, forgiving and releasing that family member from whatever retribution you've envisioned is God's solution.

2. Release discouragement

Have you ever been walking along at work or school or home, having a fantastic day, and then all of a sudden, someone says something so discouraging to you that it wrecks your day?

I've certainly experienced this many, many times throughout my life. And like I mentioned in a previous chapter, who you surround yourself with can greatly impact your life in a positive or negative way.

You see, some people enjoy planting discouraging thoughts in other people's heads just to see if they can knock others down. Some people are so wrapped up in their own pain, anger, and insecurities that they think tearing other people down will make them feel better.

Obviously as a Christ follower, we should do the opposite in our day-to-day lives and *encourage* others. But what is discouragement?

Well simply put, discouragement is the absence of courage. If you feel discouraged, it's like someone has taken your courage or, even more accurately said, like you've handed over your courage to someone else.

That last thought may sit oddly with you because we are so used to blaming others for making us feel bad. Trust me; I've heard it for over two decades as people of all types and ages have told me in my office: "It's my wife's fault that I feel bad." "It's my husband's fault that I feel bad."

"It's my kids' fault that I feel bad." "It's my parents' fault that I feel bad." "It's my boss' fault that I feel bad." (Fill in your situation here.)

Shocking as it may sound, lots of times we can feel discouraged because *we allowed* someone to plant seeds of doubt, fear, or anger in our minds.

The good news is that we can release our discouragement! We do NOT have to hold onto it. Once we realize what has happened, we can let go of the negative thoughts, forgive whoever "dropped a bomb on us," and move on with life.

And any time you feel discouragement pulling you down, I encourage you to read the Bible. Bookmark Romans 8:37 as a way to counter discouragement:

> No, in all these things we are more than conquerors
> through him who loved us. (NIV)

Filling your mind with seeds of encouragement from the Bible to counter the negativity the world throws at us every day is yet another reason you should have a dedicated time every day to read the Bible.

Remember, it's not so much what you are getting out of the Bible (although that's good); it's how much of the Bible you are getting in you!

The Original Happy Meal

In Matthew chapter 14, two of Jesus' most memorable miracles are recorded, and they show how even the disciples who were walking and talking with Jesus every day encountered dramatic highs and lows.

After speaking to a crowd of people and healing the sick all day, some of the disciples came to Jesus and advised him to dismiss the crowd and send them home because the people were hungry. Jesus responded by telling the disciples to feed the multitude, which distressed the disciples since all they could scrounge up was five small loaves of bread and two fish. That's some pretty meager pickings!

Nevertheless, Jesus blessed the tiny meal and told the disciples to distribute the food.

Now, put yourself in the place of one of those disciples. It's hot; you're tired; you're hungry; and you probably feel like Jesus has asked you to do the impossible. You've got some fragments of bread and some pieces of fish and that's it!

You look up, and there are people as far as you can see; and they're all looking at you with hungry eyes. You look back down at the scraps you've been given, shake your head, and start walking to the nearest group of people.

Suddenly, the people rush you, and you think, "They're going to trample me!"

But in the chaos, you start to notice that people are grabbing food from you and leaving with bread and fish! A cheer goes up across the crowd, and more people than you can count flock to you! "I'm going to run out!" you nervously think.

Yet, somehow, the food instantly replenishes, and people aren't leaving with the scraps you were given; they're leaving with meal-sized portions of food!

How is this possible?

By the end of this miracle, everyone present was able to eat till their bellies were full, and even after this miraculous banquet, the disciples collected TWELVE baskets of leftovers!

To this I say, "Hallelujah! God, you are able to provide for all of my needs!"

The disciples were also overjoyed with this demonstration of Jesus' power. They were stoked! I bet they were going around to each other, giving each other the ancient equivalent of high-fives and fist bumps.

They had just personally been a part of an impossible miracle, and they probably felt like nothing could ever stand in their way again. From here on out, their lives would be smooth sailing...

...or would it?

We're Sinking!

Toward the end of that *same* day, the disciples boarded a boat to take them to the other side of the lake, while Jesus stayed behind to find a secluded place to pray and recoup from the exhaustion of the day's work.

Now, place yourself once again in the place of one of the disciples. As the boat casts off, you wave to Jesus, but he's already walking toward some hills with a high overlook.

The disciples around you are excitedly retelling stories of what they experienced during the feeding of the 5,000. Peter claims that he fed more people than Andrew. Thomas rolls his eyes and says he doesn't believe it. And Judas brags that Jesus the Messiah is going to wipe out the Roman army and rule Israel as its king.

You smile, knowing that God is all-powerful and watching out for you. What could go wrong? You notice some dark clouds on the horizon as you drift off to sleep after the long day.

———————————

Suddenly, you're jarred awake by cold water splashing on your face. You spit out the water and sit up. The boat is being tossed by waves like a toy! "What's going on?!" you shout, alarmed by the water that is already sloshing around inside the boat.

Another disciple, worry written all over his face, replies, "A storm... It came out of nowhere...We keep getting pushed back out into the lake by the waves!"

You think back to Jesus walking away and feel fear and doubt creep into your heart. You look at Peter for hope, but the experienced fisherman just scowls in the darkness, unable to pilot the boat to safety.

You shout to the group over the wind and rain, "What are we going to do?"

———————

Have you ever experienced discouragement like this right after a big victory in your life? One moment, you feel like you're at the top of the world; the next moment, it's like you're in free fall.

If you're not familiar with the story of the disciples in the storm on the lake, something miraculous happened here as well. The disciples saw something like a ghost coming toward them across the lake, and it really freaked them out more than the possibility of drowning.

However, the ghost was actually Jesus walking on the water! Wow, the disciples witnessed two astounding miracles in the same day, yet they were so shaken that Jesus had to tell them, "Take courage! Don't be afraid." (NIV)

Those words from Matthew 14:27 still speak loudly to us today. When storms in our lives rise up—which they will—we should take courage in God and not give in to fear and discouragement.

Jesus performed yet another miracle during this event: he calmed the storm. The disciples all marveled at Jesus' power over the elements, but I find it really interesting that Jesus told them to take courage even before he stilled the wind.

As you take steps to make positive changes in your life, step out with courage and faith. When you meet resistance and storms, return back to Jesus' encouragement to his disciples: "Take courage! Don't be afraid."

3.   Release your failures

Remember David from point 1 in this chapter? You might think that after he was anointed by God's prophet and after he slew Goliath that it would be easy sailing for David to become king of Israel. Eventually, he even had 600 soldiers committed to his leadership, who were willing to lay down their lives for him. Surely, he could just step up to the throne and take the crown.

Well, no. You see, there was a big problem: Israel already had a king, and his name was Saul.

Worse, King Saul had already heard of David's feats and was viciously jealous, to the point that he sent a group of his soldiers to track down David and his men. This off and on hunt for David and his family lasted for about fifteen years, so David and his followers grew accustomed to having to move around a lot to stay one step ahead of the jealous King Saul.

To add to the complexity of the situation, David felt a calling from God to protect the land of Israel despite the often-murderous intentions of King Saul. On one occasion, David and his men rallied to fight back the invading army of the Amalekites and left the women and children from his camp at a town called Ziklag.

While David and his soldiers were gone, disaster struck. 1 Samuel 30:1-6 records what happened:

David and his men reached Ziklag on the third day. Now the Amalekites had raided the Negev and Ziklag. They had attacked Ziklag and burned it, and had taken captive the women and all who were in it, both young and old...When David and his men came to Ziklag, they found it destroyed by fire and their wives and sons and daughters, taken captive. So David and his men wept aloud until they had no strength left to weep...but David encouraged himself in the Lord his God. (NIV)

I can't even imagine what David and his men felt as they returned victorious in battle, just to see smoke in the distance. The town they'd left their families at for safety had been burned to the ground. It was gut wrenching!

David had made a tremendous tactical error, and once his fellow soldiers had finished weeping, they turned on David ready to stone him to death! How's that for an epic failure?!

This moment from history speaks to us today. You see, despite this horrible failure, David did something that doesn't come naturally to our minds. He praised God and encouraged himself in the Lord.

Playing the blame game doesn't help and usually just makes things worse for everyone involved. And wallowing in self-guilt is equally unproductive; it keeps you stuck in the past.

Instead of these options, David turned to God, and God protected David from his own men turning on him. David's soldiers eventually calmed and turned to the real objective at hand: rescuing their families.

With all the speed they could muster, David and most of his men pursued the Amalekites, eventually tracking them down in the countryside. After another fierce battle, David and his small army defeated the Amalekites and rescued their stolen wives and children!

So many times, we feel like our failures are going to be the end of us. I want to encourage you to think of your failures as a path to prove that God is greater than whatever failures you experience in life. In fact, God has the ability to turn your failures around into victories.

Don't believe me? Look at what 1 Samuel 30: 18-19 says:

> David recovered everything the Amalekites had taken... Nothing was missing...David brought everything back. (NIV)

Wow! Let those words encourage and inspire you the next time you are feeling the sting of a failure. With God, failures can be turned into victories.

Be an Encourager

The years of 2003 through 2007 were very stressful in my life. At times, I felt like I was in a continuous crisis at work, pastoring the church, and that heavy cloud followed me home. Stockbridge Community Church went through a long, rough transition period, and at times I didn't know if we would pull through.

Our attendance declined; our finances declined. And even though I tried my best to stay uplifted on the outside, *inside* I felt distressed, depressed, and oppressed. It seemed like everywhere I turned, my good intentions backfired.

It was during this time that I went from thinking that some of my decisions were failures to *believing* that *I* was a failure. I felt like I was drowning and nobody cared. And let me tell you, if you've been there or are currently there in that state of mind, you know it's a miserable place to be!

But here's hope for you: Just like David did in 1 Samuel 30:6, I started encouraging myself in the Lord.

You might ask me, "How do I do that, Jeff?"

In addition to countering the automatic negative thoughts I spoke about earlier, I found during this hard time that if I encouraged somebody else, I felt encouraged. You might question this, but I challenge you to try this: When you feel down, encourage three people. It can be any three people—a family member, friend, co-worker, or complete stranger.

It feels good to do good, so if you don't feel good, do good. You may chuckle or scoff at this, but I'm telling you that when I was going through a long valley of depression, it greatly brightened my day!

The next time that you need to be encouraged, encourage someone else!

Making It Personal

1. Family disappointments and hurts can be some of the deepest wounds we receive in life. From your life, what comes to mind when you hear the words *family disappointment*?

2. When you have been hurt by someone, be honest, which of these options best describes how you typically handle the pain:
   a) Replay the scenario over and over in your mind.
   b) Ignore what happened.
   c) Forgive the person who hurt you and move on.
   d) Plan how to get back at the person.

3. Read Ephesians 4:32 and Colossians 3:13. How do these verses counsel us to respond to relational hurts?

4. Discouragement can be defined as the loss of courage, confidence, or enthusiasm. Think of a time recently where you felt discouraged. What happened that led to you to feel discouraged?

5. Read Matthew 14:27. How could you use the words of Jesus in this verse to restore your courage, confidence, or enthusiasm?

6. Many times in life, it can be easy to think that just because we failed at something that we *are* a failure. How can you fight against this false idea?

7. Think of a time that you felt really down and someone encouraged you. What did they say or do that made a difference in your outlook? Does doing good make you feel good?

Chapter 8

Procrastination Elimination

*I*t's early in the morning. The sun isn't even up yet, and you're finally sleeping sweetly after a restless night. Suddenly, your alarm clock goes off, blaring this horrible noise that shatters your sleep.

Without even thinking, you fling your arm from the other side of the bed and smack the alarm clock's snooze button. And for a moment, peace returns to your bedroom.

Five minutes later, just as you were starting to slip back into dreamland, the alarm on your cell phone goes off.

UGH!

You feel across the surface of the lampstand next to your bed and find your phone. After a few unhappy taps at its screen, the alarm snoozes, and you sink back into your pillow under the warm covers.

BEEP! BEEP! BEEP!

It's been nine minutes, and now your original alarm clock is going off again. You think of hitting the snooze button once more. You swallow, and your throat feels scratchy. You flirt with the idea of calling in sick, but you don't have a fever, and you know you're not sick. You just want to go back to bed.

By now, the alarm on your cell phone has started blaring again, joining your alarm clock in this horribly irritating chorus. With a big grunt of "FINE", you silence the alarms, throw off your covers, and roll out of bed.

You know you're already running late, so you shuffle into your bathroom, pick up the toothpaste tube, and give it a good squeeze. But instead of just loading up your toothbrush, a string of toothpaste shoots out onto the counter and sink. You shake your head, "I'll clean it up later."

You jump into the shower, intending to hurry, but you find that the warm water is lulling you into slow motion. You wish you could just crawl back into bed, but you manage to snap yourself out of a trance and finish showering and getting ready. Tossing on most of your clothes, you hurry to the kitchen, the rest of your clothes trailing along.

Flipping on the news as you rush to the pantry, you hear that there's been a bad accident on the highway and that traffic is backed up for miles. "Great," you sigh as you rummage around the pantry shelves. Your stomach grumbles in anticipation of being fed, but you're unable to find any breakfast bars or quick breakfast items. "I should've gotten groceries yesterday."

You glance at a box of cereal but shake your head. "I don't have time for that now."

And a look at the clock in the lower screen of the news channel confirms your statement.

Giving up on breakfast, you grab your car keys and head straight for your car. Sinking into your car's seat, you start it up and then wonder, "Did I lock the door?"

But there's no time, so you throw the car in reverse and start your commute. And as you drive the morning route you are so accustomed to, it's like the slowest drivers in the world all suddenly want to be in front of you!

All the time, you keep glancing at the clock on the car's dashboard. Your heart is pounding; you know your blood pressure is up in the clouds somewhere; and you finally come to grips with the fact that you're going to be late...again.

———————

Ever experienced something like this?

I'm sure that most of you have experienced something like this, and for some of you, this *is* your regular morning routine. But I'm not judging you. Trust me, this story is very much like *my* old morning routine.

It's crazy how something so small as saying, "I'll do it later," or repeatedly hitting the snooze bar on your alarm can pile pressure on ourselves later.

Procrastination—the act of putting things off—can set a negative tone for our day and for our life.

I used to be really bad at putting things off. I don't even know where I learned to do this because my mother and father tackled the hard stuff instead of avoiding it. But it took me a long time to break this habit of waiting till the last minute to get things done, and I'd like to share with you how I broke this bad habit in the hope that it will help you.

1. Be filled with God's Spirit

By my teenage years, I was very undisciplined in school. In fact, my only objective in school was to get *out* of school! At that time, I didn't realize that I had attention-deficit disorder. All I knew was that I couldn't focus for a long period of time and was terrible at reading.

The summer before my freshman year, I became a follower of Jesus Christ. That was also the summer that I met Rhonda, and we became high school sweethearts.

After becoming a Christian, I suddenly wanted to know more about God and to develop a relationship with him. It was an inner feeling that kept pulling me to him.

Thankfully, my father and stepmother bought me my first Bible. Despite my difficulty with reading, I opened up my Bible and started reading. I even accidentally freaked out my stepmother one day when she entered my bedroom unannounced and found me lying on my bed reading the Bible! She was overjoyed and shocked at the same time.

Discipleship Class

At church, my student pastor, Randy Brooks, was starting a discipleship class on Sundays. It required a lot of Bible reading and Scripture memorization. I wanted to join but hesitated, thinking about whether I'd be able to keep up with everyone else. But I knew that it would help me as a young Christian to learn more about the Bible and about God, so I threw caution to the wind and joined.

To my delight, Rhonda joined the class as well!

Over the next series of weeks, I read the assigned Bible passages, did the homework for class, and studied for the end of unit test. Yes, *me*, the guy who hated reading, doing homework, and taking tests!

A transformation was taking place inside of my heart, my mind, and my life. It was *change* in the best way.

Throughout the discipleship class, Rhonda and I were in a back-and-forth competition for the top spot in the class. In the end, Rhonda scored just a little bit higher than me, but that didn't bother me, because I liked her a lot anyway, plus I was amazed by how I was changing.

For the first time in a long time, I actually cared about doing my best in something. It was like the sunrise of a new day, and I wanted to become better. I started thinking about where else I could improve.

Prior to my conversion, I started high school with the mindset of just getting by. I tallied up the minimum class credits I needed to graduate and set a goal of reaching that number and no more.

I remember having to take a world history class even though I didn't need the credits. So I didn't do any of the work for the class. While everyone else in the class feverishly took notes, I just sat there. I didn't turn in assignments, and I certainly didn't study for the tests. Thus, my grade in the class was a *30*, and I deserved it.

But in the middle of that year was when I accepted Jesus as my Savior and when my thinking and actions began to change. David, one of my friends from middle school, came up to me one day in the hall at school and asked, "What's wrong with you?"

At first, I thought he was mad at me for something, but he continued with, "First, you don't curse anymore and now you're on the A B Honor Roll!"

This was the first time I got to share about my faith in Jesus with someone.

And David wasn't the only one who had noticed a change in me. My teachers began to ask me about the reversal in behavior, and I told them about how I had turned my life over to God. I became known as "The Guy Who's a Christian."

Looking back, I realize that it was God's Holy Spirit who was helping me transform my life. And the evidence was in the "fruit of the Spirit" as described in Galatians 5:22-23 that was being produced through my words and actions:

> But the fruit of the Spirit is love, joy, peace, patience, kindness, goodness, faithfulness, gentleness and self-control. Against such things there is no law. (NIV)

These wonderful attributes grow in the life of a person who has chosen to follow Jesus. And in the context of procrastination and my high school turn around, take a look at the last fruit of the Spirit listed in the verse above.

As a Christian, with the Holy Spirit inside of you, *self-control* is available to you. You actually have an advantage in being able to change to make your life better when compared with those who do not follow Jesus.

You might say to this statement, "Hang on, Jeff; I know plenty of athletes and musicians and business people who are extremely disciplined but definitely don't live like Jesus."

To this, I respond with, "Yes."

You see, God has blessed us with a brain with the freedom of thought and decision, and anyone can choose to discipline themselves if they truly want to. Olympic athletes are the epitome of this. They spend their lives training, eating right, competing, and pushing their bodies to the limit of what is humanly possible.

Now, I'm not saying that with the Holy Spirit, you're going to suddenly wake up one morning and run a marathon in record time...and please don't try to unless you've trained for it. What I'm saying is that with the help of the Holy Spirit, self-control can come *more naturally* and more easily for anyone following Jesus.

Going back to our Olympians as examples, I've heard and read many stories throughout the years of extraordinary athletes who have won many medals in competitions but whose personal lives are a sad wreck.

And it's not just athletes who face this problem of being successful in one arena but whose lives may be falling apart out of the public eye. We all struggle with issues and sins—even Christians.

The difference here is that Christians have the Holy Spirit, and the Holy Spirit will empower us to do what is right and discourage us from doing what is wrong. The Holy Spirit becomes our conscience, louder and more informative than the conscience God built into the human mind.

The Holy Spirit gives direction and acts as our mentor on our journey of change to become more like Jesus. And according to Romans 8:26, the Holy Spirit helps us in our weakness.

I thank God for giving his followers the Holy Spirit! He makes a noticeable change in our lives like 2 Corinthians 5:17 describes:

> Anyone who belongs to Christ is a new person. The past
> is forgotten, and everything is new. (CEV)

Hallelujah! Our past can be forgotten, and we can walk a new life through the transforming power of God!

2. Do what is most important

At age twenty-six, I became a pastor, and being a pastor is like being self-employed. I didn't have someone telling me what I needed to get done every day. I worked hard at whatever I did, but I also found myself putting off the important things.

For a preacher, one of the highest priorities during a week is to prepare Sunday's message. Every week, I knew that Sunday was coming. As I was out visiting and praying for the sick, I always had in the back of my mind, "You gotta work on that message."

I'd start putting down on paper my thoughts for the week's sermon, and the phone would ring. It would be another pastor checking on me or a church member wanting to tell me about something very important to them or any number of other people wanting to speak to me in that very moment when I was trying to write my sermon. And you know what, I confess that I was more than happy to talk to them because deep down inside, I really didn't want to study or write the message!

As the days of the week wore on, the tension inside of me started growing. I knew that Sunday would eventually arrive, and I couldn't just stand on stage without a message. But I'd take every opportunity given to me to push back the time I worked on my sermon.

"I can work on it tomorrow," I'd tell myself. And then the next day, I'd say, "I'll do it tomorrow."

Have you ever told yourself that?

Still No Message

By the weekend, I'd still have no message, and my anxiety level was high! Worse, I couldn't even enjoy the weekend with my family because I was so irritable and at times panicked. What a terrible atmosphere for trying to write a message!

And if yard work or house repairs or a special dinner meeting came up on Saturday, I felt like the pressure was enough to push me over a cliff. More times than I'd like to admit, I would be up late at night and into the early morning hours putting together my sermon for that day.

This unhealthy cycle continued for several years, and I hated it. Yet, I was the one creating it, and I felt miserable.

You might ask me, "Where was the Holy Spirit during this time? Wasn't he helping you develop self-control?"

I'd simply answer that the Holy Spirit *was with me* the whole time, prodding me to start writing the sermon on Monday, reminding me to do it on Tuesday, prompting me to write it on Wednesday and on the rest of the days of the week as well. He was helping me develop self-control in my life, but when it came to this stronghold of writing the Sunday message, I was IGNORING him.

A funny thing about God is that you can try to ignore him, but he will eventually get your attention.

The Enlightening Breakfast

One day, my good friend Chad Smith, who had also become a pastor, invited me to breakfast at Cracker Barrel. On the phone, he excitedly said, "Jeff, I want to show you something that has changed my life!" I was intrigued.

Upon arriving and being seated, we placed our order, and then Chad leaned over to his book bag and pulled out a medium-sized, brown notebook. I was puzzled and disappointed at the same time. I thought, "Man, you have wasted my time."

But then he began explaining how this little notebook had revolutionized his life. He had attended a Franklin Covey time-management seminar. He opened the notebook and began showing me how he had started planning out his day ahead of time and how he prioritized the most important tasks.

At first, looking at all of Chad's notes divided by time made my eyes swim. But the concept really grabbed my attention, so much so, that not long after this enlightening breakfast, I attended the same time-management seminar by Franklin Covey and learned to do what is important first.

In the class, we learned a powerful illustration that I'd like to share with you.

The Impossible Fish Bowl

Picture a small fish bowl with clear glass. Now picture someone filling a fourth of the bowl with sand. Next add small chunks of gravel to another fourth. Follow this by adding six golf balls.

Wow, by now, your imagined fish bowl should be getting very full. So when I ask you to add three baseballs to the bowl, you should shake your head and say it's not possible. You try to ram three in there, but you can only get one. The other two will just have to sit neglected.

In this mental exercise, the three baseballs represent the three highest-priority things that you must get done on that day. The golf balls are important tasks that need to be done that day but not as important as the top three. The gravel symbolizes important things that are not time sensitive, like planning an event in the future. And the sand represents things that are not important at all to your day's work, like scrolling through social media.

And that's the illustration of the Impossible Fish Bowl.

But...what if I told you that there's a way to fit everything into the fish bowl?

Reimagine with me the empty, glass fish bowl. This time, let's start by putting the biggest items in first. Place the three baseballs in the bowl. They easily fit.

Now, add the six golf balls. One, two, three, four, five, six. Yep, they all fit. Add the gravel. Stone by stone, they sink into the vacant spaces around the larger objects. And finally, take a look at the pile of sand left to add. Do you think it will all fit?

As you start adding the sand, what happens? Because the sand is actually just a lot of small grains, it slides down into the many voids left by the other objects. And before you know it, you've filled the Impossible Fish Bowl!

What you've just seen in your own mind is that by getting the most important things of the week out of the way first, you will have plenty of time to work through the rest of the week's tasks.

After learning this simple yet profound principle, I started applying it to lots of areas of my life and particularly to my Sunday message. Since this is one of the highest priorities of my week, I now work on it for two hours a day, first thing in the morning, Monday through Thursday.

Not only have my messages gotten much better thanks to this technique, but I also get to enjoy rest on Friday and serve in our community on Saturday without the stress of an impending deadline.

Ephesians 5:15-17 advises us to:

> Be careful how you live. Do not be unwise but wise, making the best use of your time because the times are evil. Therefore, do not be foolish, but understand what the Lord's will is. (NIV)

I challenge you to make a list each week or even each day. On this list, simply write the most important things you need to accomplish. Then by each item, write a 1 by the top priority, a 2 by the next important, and a 3 by the third most important.

Just focus on three things. Remember putting the baseballs in the fish bowl? I promise you that if you make this a regular part of your routine, you're going to be amazed at how much more you can accomplish in the same amount of time it took you to do less. And as a bonus, it will open up more free time for you. To me that screams, "Win-win."

I dare you to give it a try!

3.   Go deeper to live in peace

What if you could relieve some of the stress you feel each week that arises from uncertainty? Maybe you'd feel more energized during your day. Perhaps you'd feel more creative or more relaxed than you normally would.

Well, here's the secret to helping make this happen in your life, and it works in conjunction with what you just learned.

Once you've given all your weekly tasks a priority, there's one more simple but often forgotten step to really take control of your tasks and time: Move your tasks from a piece of paper to your calendar.

Whether you use a paper calendar, the calendar on your phone, or an online calendar like Google, assigning your tasks beginning with the "three baseballs" to a specific day and time can immediately relieve some of the stress you've been carrying around with you throughout the week.

As long as you follow the schedule that *you* are setting, you'll know when you're going to work on the most important stuff for the week, and that frees you from the worry of uncertainty. Another bonus side effect from scheduling your most important tasks is that you will suddenly find free time!

If you just wing your work days and week, improvising your schedule as you go along, chances are extremely high that you end up wasting time switching back and forth among your tasks, trying to decide what you should do next. Add some procrastination in there, and you can easily pile a whole bunch of stress on yourself.

What would it be like if instead of having to stay late at work to finish your tasks, you had more free time to spend with your family?

A word of caution here: If you're able to carve out more free time from your schedule, protect it! I don't know how people find out, but it seems like every time I've set aside time from my schedule for family or reading or writing or serving in the community or just relaxing on a bench outside admiring creation, everyone wants that time.

People text, call, try to Facetime, visit, and so on. If you've intentionally set aside time for quiet, I highly recommend you silence your phone or leave it in a safe place. And don't take a computer or tablet with you.

If you have children, consider how much time you want to give up to extracurricular activities during the week. Now I know that some of you reading this have very active families, with children in sports, ballet, gymnastics, quilting—okay, maybe not quilting—throughout the week. And that might work well with your family.

I've also seen lots of parents who rarely see their children because after subtracting time for school, homework, activities, and dinner (somewhere in there), the day is gone. Worse, I've seen spouses drift apart as one takes this child to some activity and the other spouse takes another child to a different activity almost every night of the week. These families just didn't spend time together anymore, and that can be dangerous for the stability of a marriage and for the family as a whole.

Tumbling Mats

When my daughter Katelyn was young, Rhonda and I registered her in a gymnastics program at a local gym. It was just one night a week, which worked great for our schedule; plus, Katelyn had an absolute blast stretching and tumbling on the mats along with the other kids.

She was having fun; it was relatively inexpensive; and we still had other time during the week to have dinners together and play games.

And then one day, her coach approached Rhonda and me and recommended that Katelyn join the traveling gymnastics team. At first, the offer sounded great. Katelyn was jumping-up-and-down happy, and Rhonda and I were impressed that the coach believed our daughter had the level of talent required to compete.

But then we got out the calendar and started realizing what this offer was going to cost. Either Rhonda or I would have to travel with Katelyn on Saturdays and various nights during the weeks. Sometimes the competitions would require stay overs at a hotel.

Rhonda and I talked it over for a while, because we both knew how much Katelyn loved gymnastics. But eventually, we both arrived at the same conclusion: Travel gymnastics would not be good for our family.

So we had to break the news to Katelyn, and she was heartbroken. I remember watching her cry and thinking, "This is for the best." But, man, it was tough!

And she hasn't let us forget our decision either. Even though it's been many years since our decision, every time we watch the Olympics on TV, she'll suddenly point to the screen at a gymnast on the American team and just shake her head while sighing, "That could've been me."

So if you're thinking right now that I'm a terrible parent, let me share with you the rest of the story. You see, Katelyn was okay at gymnastics, but she had a strong talent in music and singing that was just starting to develop.

She stopped gymnastics and started pursuing music. She auditioned for the Spivey Hall Children's Choir and was accepted into their program! Rhonda and I taxied her to the weekly practices, and as I sat out in the audience and listened to her sing with the choir, I remember thinking, "Yes! Katelyn, *this* is your talent!"

And you know what, she believed it in her heart, too!

She ended up going into a college music program and graduated with a degree in music. She learned to play piano and bass, and I love to hear her sing.

Parents, I encourage you to use the wisdom you've gained through your life's experiences to help guide your children. And by all means, don't let other people decide your family's calendar. *You* decide what goes on your calendar and be sure to plan things for your family to do together!

In fact, someone reading this just pulled up the calendar on their phone and scheduled a family game night for Saturday. Good on you!

And don't forget God. Be sure to put time for God on your calendar. For me, he's the first appointment I add to my daily schedule. Why? If it's the first thing you do, you won't run out of time during the day to do it! Guaranteeing a special time of devotion with God every day in your schedule will somehow make a lot of the other pieces of your schedule fit into place.

Always remember this promise from Jesus in Matthew 6:33:

> But seek first the kingdom of God and his righteousness,
> and all these things will be given to you as well. (NIV)

Eliminating Procrastination = Greatly Reduced Stress and a New You

If you are a parent, I encourage you to talk over with your spouse how much time you'd like to spend together as a family during the week. And do something fun together.

And, hey, put your family time on your calendar. If it matters to you, you should put it on your calendar! Save your new-found time for things that you truly value.

Making It Personal

1. Thinking back over the past few weeks at home, school, or work, do you find yourself tackling some tasks quickly and postponing others? What do you find easy to work on? What tasks would you put off forever if you could?

2. Looking at your answers to the previous questions, how could you change your thinking about what you frequently try to avoid?

3. Read Ephesians 5:15-17. How do these verses advise us to live? How would you apply these words to your own life and the decisions that you make each day?

4. To live a more fulfilling life, what weekly/monthly activities are eating up your time or pulling the enjoyment out of your life? How difficult would it be to remove these from your schedule?

5. Flipping the last question, what fun activities could you add to your monthly calendar that would benefit you and your family?

6. The next time that you are tempted to put off doing something that is very important, how could you inspire yourself to tackle the task head on? Remember that eliminating procrastination can greatly reduce stress in your life.

7. We schedule appointments, meetings, events, and many other things on our calendar. Have you ever scheduled time with God on your calendar? If you have never done this, give it a try for a week. It could be a good method to help you stay consistent in spending time with God daily.

Chapter 9

Patience

*H*ow patient a person would you say you are? Very patient? Sort of patient? Not very patient?

If you're at a standstill in a traffic jam on the freeway, do you think, "God, thank you for this wonderful moment to just breathe deeply and think of your goodness and release all my concerns to you," or are you more like, "If these cars don't get out of my way, I'm going to drive over all of them!"

I believe that most of us in this situation would probably feel a lot more like the second statement than the first, not that we would actually drive over the cars in front of us. I certainly feel a lot more like the second one because, true confession, I struggle with patience.

I wonder a lot if I will become more patient as I get older. As I'm writing this chapter, I'm 52, and I can tell you with a laugh that patience is *not* automatically coming to me with age!

I don't know if people are born naturally patient or impatient, but I do know that when both of my children were born, they were definitely impatient when it came to being fed and needing a diaper change! They loudly let Rhonda and me know they wanted food or a change NOW!

When I think back to the home life I grew up in, I know that I also learned a lot of impatient behavior from my parents. My mom and dad divorced early in my life, so this meant that forever on, holidays like Thanksgiving would be spent with me traveling to one house and then the other—which can be stressful if both parents are impatient.

For Thanksgiving each year, we settled upon visiting my dad on the Sunday evening before Thanksgiving and visiting with my mom for lunch on Thanksgiving Day. And even though Rhonda and I have been punctually following this schedule for years, I still get a call on Sunday from my dad thirty minutes before our arrival time, saying, "Hey, Jeff, where are you at?"

And on Thanksgiving Thursday, Mom calls about thirty minutes before our arrival time, asking, "Jeff, where you? We're about ready to start!" It's become so predictably comical that I look over at Rhonda as we're heading to each of their houses and say, "Now you watch; they're gonna call any moment." And sure enough, like clockwork, there's the call.

My parents are impatient, and I am, too. But you know what; it's not their fault I lack patience. I'm an adult who has the freedom to choose my thoughts, actions, and words, so I am responsible for my struggle with impatience.

"Don't Pray for That!"

In my early years of following Jesus, I started recognizing that my impatience was a problem. I had learned that one of the fruits of the Spirit is patience and that God is very patient with us (Hallelujah!).

Since I wanted to be more like Jesus, I innocently asked a preacher, "Should I pray for patience?"

His face instantly paled and expression changed as he took a step back from me as if I'd told him that I had leprosy! With one of his fingers shaking in my face, he scolded, "Don't ever pray for that! If you do, everything in your life will become aggravating!"

"Wow," I thought. "I'm glad I asked. I guess I won't be praying for patience."

But you know what, I don't agree with what I was told anymore. Sure, praying for patience may bring more time delays into your life, but it's experiencing and peacefully overcoming them that builds patience within a person!

My Time Is More Important!

Over the years, I've also had another realization about impatience: It comes out of *selfishness*.

Now, you might disagree with me here, but maybe you've noticed in your own life that some delays don't really bother you that much and other delays may make you so mad that you're ready to literally explode!

What was it about the ones that really sent you overboard that triggered your reaction? Were you feeling pressured that you needed to be somewhere else at a particular time, with people waiting for you, but a traffic jam blew out whatever patience you had? Maybe you were the other person, waiting for someone else who ended up being an hour late, and they said it was because they were stuck in traffic, but you were like, "Google Maps shows that the road was clear."

Maybe you skipped lunch one day, because work was extremely busy, and you were very hungry, so you stopped by a fast-food restaurant to pick up dinner on the way home, and it took forever for you to get your food. This was terrible customer service, of course, but how did you wait through the delay to get your food? Did you open a book and start reading in the drive through, or did you start honking on the car horn? (I confess; I have honked on the horn in a drive through before.)

Maybe you broke in line at a store during the Christmas shopping season—you know, when the lines go all the way to the back of the store. I actually witnessed a person break in line at a Walmart one year, and it got ugly fast! Merry Christmas.

The point I'm trying to make here is that patience is being able to accept delays.

Sure, if you've been waiting for your order at a fast-food place for twenty minutes, go remind them that you're still waiting. They may have lost your order; it's happened to me. And if you've been standing at a ticket counter at the airport for assistance for a while and no one seems to want to help you, speak up for yourself and find someone to help you.

But can you accept delays?

How long a wait would it take to transform you from a sensible, calm person into a child throwing a full-on tantrum? Three hours in line at the latest Disney World attraction? Two hours waiting for a bus that should've been there in thirty minutes? Ten minutes in the drive through line at Starbucks?

Patience or impatience. Our everyday lives force us to choose how we'll react to the settings that really "try our patience." And, oh boy, there are some things that really test my patience.

You Overcharged Us!

When I first became the pastor of what would later become Stockbridge Community Church, we met in a tiny building. I inherited how things had been done by the previous pastor.

My clerk, Sister Hays, at the time was eighty years old, and she would keep our tiny budget on a yellow legal pad. It's crazy to me now that our church's entire weekly budget fit on just seven lines of her legal pad. She'd write in either black or red ink to show whether an item was in the positive or negative.

On one morning, she tapped the legal pad with her pen and said that we were in the negative because our insurance company had made a mistake and overcharged us a hundred dollars.

Well, I puffed out my chest and assured my clerk that I'd take care of this problem right then. So I went into my small office, whipped the phone receiver up to my ear, and punched in the telephone number to our insurance company representative.

When he didn't answer, I left a very curt message saying that he needed to return my call as soon as possible.

Two days passed, and I still hadn't heard from our insurance rep. I went into my budget meeting with Sister Hays, and with raised eyebrows, she inquired about the insurance error, tapping at the numbers on her legal pad. I squirmed a little, because I had promised her that I'd take care of the problem.

Now, I was feeling both a little bit embarrassed and also angry that our insurance company hadn't returned my call. I was frustrated that they weren't being prompt about an error on their side. I can assure you that if we suddenly stopped paying our bill that we'd hear from them pretty quickly.

Over the next three weeks, I left a string of voicemail messages, each one being more and more irritated and angry in tone. Finally, I was getting ready to drive over to our insurance rep's office to give him a piece of my mind when I thought that I'd give him one more call.

To my shock, our insurance representative answered!

"Hello?" he unemotionally said.

I had been waiting for this moment, and I wanted him to feel exactly what I'd been feeling for the past three weeks.

"Yes, this is Jeff Daws, pastor of Forest Park Church of God, and I've been trying to get in touch with you for three weeks now, and I haven't heard back from you yet!"

Silence.

"And let me tell you that if you treat your customers like this, sir, you aren't going to stay in business long! In fact, we might be looking for another insurance company because of you not returning my calls and the fact that we were overcharged $100!"

There was another pause on the line, and then I could hear our rep draw in a deep breath before responding in a distraught voice.

"Sir, I apologize for not responding to your voicemails in a timely manner..."

He trailed off, and then continued.

"...Sir, my house burned down during that time period, and I've lost everything."

Wham! I felt like a ton of bricks just dropped from the sky onto me.

He said, "I'm sorry that your big problem of being overcharged a hundred dollars has devastated your life. My life has been turned upside down, and I'm trying to piece my life back together."

Now, it was my turn to be silent.

He finished with, "I've already put in the request to have your account adjusted to fix our mistake. So, is there anything else I can do for you today?"

To say that I felt humbled is a huge understatement.

I know it's not right for businesses to overcharge their customers, nor is it right for a business to ignore its customers. But I think that many times, we forget that the person on the other end of the phone or behind the store counter is a *person*.

Impatience can easily fool us into thinking that having to wait is a *personal attack* directly on us. In reality, the people we deal with every day are having to juggle their own tasks, worries, and concerns hidden behind the scenes. Please think about that the next time you are inconvenienced.

I WANT That!

So at this point, you might be thinking, "Yeah, Jeff, I know I can be really impatient sometimes. But if I want to change, how do I do it?"

Building on the idea that impatience is tied to selfishness, the next time you feel anger rising inside of you because you're having to wait for someone or something, STOP.

Stop whatever you were thinking about and doing and ask yourself, "Am I being selfish because I'm not getting what I want right now? Am I acting like a reasonable person or like a little child throwing a tantrum at Walmart because they're not getting the toy they wanted?"

I think back on so many "tantrums" I've thrown in life as an adult who was being impatient, and I wish I could go back and tell myself to stop and ask myself those questions. Had I done that, I believe that the end results would have been much better all around.

You see, I believe in treating people with respect, and I want to lead as many people to Jesus as I can. But I tell you this: When I've lost my patience in public in the past, I've also lost the ability to be a witness for Jesus to them.

For the longest time, I didn't get that. But we can't be better or do better until we know better, and now, I know better. So now, I'm much more intentional about staying patient, even though I have to wait.

Cracking the Code

In the Bible, "patience" appears in a really interesting place. You may have heard verses from 1 Corinthians chapter 13 read in a wedding, but it's more than just for a wedding service. Chapter 13 defines biblical love, and verses 4 and 5 connect with *patience*. Take a look at the following:

> Love is patient, love is kind. It does not envy, it does not boast, it is not proud. It is not rude, it is not self-seeking, it is not easily angered, it keeps no record of wrongs. (NIV)

Wow! Part of the definition of *love* is being *patient*. If we want to be more loving to someone, we must be more patient with them. When we start becoming impatient, we must remember that our love is being tested, not just our patience.

I'm not saying that you're never going to get upset with someone. Even Jesus got upset with people who were ripping off others in the Temple marketplace.

Patience helps you stay in control when you feel like getting *out of* control. And, think with me, showing love to others helps them to relax. Showing love to others lowers stress and anger. Patient love builds bridges among people.

Patience is a fruit of the Spirit as mentioned in Galatians 5:22-23. Patience should grow out of your life as your relationship with God grows.

Patience also grows by you encountering situations that "test" your patience. If you go to a gym and work out, your muscles only grow when they repeatedly encounter resistance. That's part of the work that you have to put into getting into shape. If all you had to do to be ripped was sit on a couch all day, everybody would be in fantastic shape.

In reality, it takes consistent work to build up your muscles. In the same way, our daily interactions with people give us countless opportunities to grow our patience.

By now, you're probably like, "I get it, Jeff. I need to be more patient. But what are some specific ways for me to do that?"

I'm glad you asked! I'm going to share with you three specific steps that have really helped me to grow my patience.

How to Grow Your Patience

If you want to experience real change in your life that produces patience start with this pillar of patience:

1. **Lower your expectations of people; raise your expectations of God**

Since the overwhelming majority of times that your patience is tried involves others, let's start there. Would you agree with me that most of us place high expectations on others and that when they don't live up to our expectations, we get very impatient with them?

Another question: How many times have you actually told these people exactly what you were expecting?

If you're like most people, you've probably told a few people, like some co-workers, family, or friends, a few of your expectations. You've told them certain things that you like and don't like. You may have communicated the most important things that need to be done for a work project. Your family and friends probably know the restaurants or food that you don't like, and they probably know the ones you love.

However, if you're like most people, including me, you're probably holding a whole secret list of unspoken expectations by which you judge everyone who is in your day-to-day life. For some of you, this secret list is as huge as a dictionary or even a set of encyclopedias!

Think with me here: If we tell people our expectations, it takes the guesswork and potential frustration and disappointment out of a lot of situations.

I can see the wheels turning in your mind right now, and you might have thought, "Yeah, but what happens when people don't follow through with what I've told them, or what if they've told me that they were going to do something and they don't?"

To grow your patience and relationships, I say to lower your expectations of people, and to raise your expectations of God.

Too many times, we treat people like a god, expecting them to read our minds or snap a finger and make us happy. This statement may sound obvious, but judging by the way that humans treat each other, they keep forgetting that people are not God! Only God is God! Raise your expectations on what he can do in your life.

Listen to how James 5:8 says we should live:

You, too, must be patient, for the coming of the Lord
is near. (NLT)

Your situation may be out of your control, but it is not out of God's
control. God is always working even when you don't see him working.
Raise your expectations on God by talking to him more. Pray to God
daily and share with him everything that is bothering you. The Bible
tells us in 1 Peter 5:7:

Give all your worries and cares to God, for he cares
about you. (NLT)

By lowering your expectations of people and raising your expectations of God, you will be on your way to increasing your patience
throughout the day.

2. Avoid complaining while waiting

When we are being forced to wait, we need to watch how we are
talking with our mouth out loud and what we're saying in our mind!
James 5:9 says:

Don't grumble about each other, brothers and sisters,
or you will be judged. (NLT)

Waiting can be frustrating, especially when things don't go how we
pictured them. At that point, we frequently start looking for someone
to blame. Now remember, I discussed earlier about how the root of
impatience is selfishness. Blaming others isn't going to get you through

the checkout line any faster, but it will certainly make you miserable while you wait.

Here's a question for you: Do you find yourself complaining a lot throughout the day?

In the morning, do you rise or whine? Do you hit the ground smiling or griping? If you come home dog-tired from work, is it because you growled all day long?

Complaining is draining. It drains you of a joyful life. And, hey, complaining is easy! It's like our human "default setting" to just complain if we can't have our way. But it's like I always say: Complaining is like bad breath; you only notice it when it comes out of someone else's mouth!

In Psalm 141:3, the Psalmist prayed:

> Set a guard over my mouth, O Lord; keep watch over
> the door of my lips. (NIV)

Don't be like the wife who griped at her husband for most of their married life. When he died, she put on his tombstone, "Rest in Peace." And then came the reading of the will. The husband left his wife $5 and everything else to his secretary. Afterward, the wife added to her husband's tombstone, "Till we meet again!"

Avoid complaining.

3. Wait confidently on God

As my children grew up, I noticed that they had a hard time distinguishing between "no" and "not yet." And actually, I think most people have a hard time separating those two responses.

Patience is a trait of being a mature Christian. Babies always want whatever it is they want immediately, but a mature person can wait.

Let me share with you this important principle of prayer:

When we ask God for something and we don't get it immediately, we may think the answer is "no," but many times the answer is actually "not yet."

God will not give you something that you're not ready for yet. God loves to bless his children, but through his omniscience he also knows what will turn into a curse if he were to give it to you. Many times, we must grow in our walk with God and become a more mature follower of Christ before we can receive what we are asking for.

And quite frankly, God knows far better than we do how to bless us. We may anguish, praying for something for a long time and wondering if God is hearing us, when behind the scenes, he wants to bless us with something so much better than we can imagine.

So waiting on God is one of the chief characteristics of being a Christian. James 5:10-11 says:

> My friends, follow the example of the prophets who spoke for the Lord. They were patient, even when they had to suffer...You may remember how patient Job was and how the Lord finally helped him. The Lord did this because he is so merciful and kind. (CEV)

Job lost everything of value that he owned in one day! Yet, he kept his faith in God and refused to complain or curse at God for all of the horrible things that happened to him. Job put his trust in God and patiently waited for God to restore him. It was a long miserable wait. Job even broke out in boils all over his body and had to endure the questioning of his friends, who were completely convinced that Job had done something terribly wrong to deserve his tragedy. But in the end, God showed up and rewarded Job by blessing him with much more than he originally had.

You may be waiting on God right now for the answer to a prayer. I encourage you to stay in there with your faith and patience as you wait. God's answer may be "not yet."

There's a fantastic description of God and his promise for us related to patience in Isaiah 40:28-31. Take a look at it:

> Have you not known? Have you not heard? The everlasting God, the Lord, the Creator of the ends of the earth, neither faints nor is weary. His understanding is unsearchable. He gives power to the weak, and to those who have no might he increases strength...those who wait on the Lord shall renew their strength; they shall mount up with wings like eagles, they shall run and not be weary, they shall walk and not faint. (NKJV)

"Those who wait on the Lord." Practicing patience with God moves you from being a "Chicken" Christian to an "Eagle" Christian. No, I'm not calling anyone names here. I'm pointing to the difference between chickens and eagles.

Think about how a chicken behaves. It spends its days walking around the barnyard with its head down, pecking and scratching at the ground, trying to find food. This reminds me of people who live in a "victim" mindset. They say and think things like, "Everyone else has it better than me. I'll never get ahead. So and so always gets the good breaks."

When a storm comes, the chickens all panic and run for the chicken coup for shelter. Notice that the verse in Isaiah doesn't say that God would mount up on chicken wings.

Unlike the chicken, the eagle spends much time soaring high in the air, scanning the world below for opportunities. Its acute vision allows it to focus in on potential food far below. And during storms, it can spread its wings out and allow the air currents to lift it even higher.

I don't know about you, but I much rather be like an eagle than like a chicken! I encourage you to stop running with the "chickens" and start letting the wind of God's Spirit lift you up while you patiently wait for the answers to your prayers.

Just like Habakkuk 2:3 assures:

> These things won't happen right away. Slowly, steadily, surely, the time approaches when the vision will be fulfilled. If it seems slow, do not despair, for these things will surely come to pass. Just be patient! They will not be overdue a single day! (TLB)

Lower your expectations of people and raise your expectations of God. Avoid complaining while you wait. And wait confidently on God. Building these three pillars in your life will grow and strengthen your patience.

And like the eagle embraces the storm, learn to embrace being inconvenienced in your everyday life as a way to give your patience a workout. I promise you, if you haven't already had a chance to practice your patience today, it's coming. So make use of it!

Making It Personal

1. How patient would say you are? (Be honest.)

2. When was a time recently that your patience was tested?

3. In what types of situations do you find your patience tried to its limit?

4. In the future, when you realize that your patience is failing, what could you do to de-escalate the situation?

5. Read 1 Corinthians 13:4-7. How are love and patience interrelated?

6. How often would you say that God has been patient with you in your life? Have you ever had any moments in your life where you wondered if God was going to give up on you?

7. Read Isaiah 40:31. According to this verse, what benefits are there in worshipping the Lord while you wait?

Chapter 10

The Gratitude Attitude

*H*ave you ever been in an elevator and thought about how it worked?

Rhonda loves going to New York City. She loves the buildings, the energy, the excitement. She especially loves to take a tour of the city at night, when the city transforms from a bunch of gray and glass buildings into a beautifully lit fairyland of lights.

On one particular trip, we were riding up to the top of the Empire State Building to view the city from above. It was during that moment, as our elevator car shot upward, higher and higher, that I thought about small things being really important. I thought about the cable, supporting the weight of our very full elevator car. I thought about the wheels along the side that would (hopefully) brake and lock into place to protect us if the cable should break.

Of course, while I'm thinking about this, I look over at Rhonda, and she's having a great time, delighted to see the city skyline below. Thankfully, we had no issues going up or down, but I can assure you that small things matter.

Houston, We Have a Problem

In 1999, all eyes in NASA's mission control were on the monitors showing the progress of the *Mars Climate Orbiter*. The scientists were thrilled with the potential to study Mars with this new $125-million satellite platform. After months of travel to the red planet, the orbiter arrived and abruptly stopped sending messages.

Even though the scientists tried everything they could think of to reestablish contact with the orbiter, they never heard from it again. A later investigation revealed that the orbiter had misunderstood where it needed to enter orbit and instead disintegrated in the atmosphere.

And do you know what caused this space disaster? A small mathematical error. One of the companies that worked on the project used the imperial system of measurement (inches), and the other used the metric system (centimeters). And someone, somewhere forgot to convert!

I think NASA would definitely agree that small things matter!

Another math error gave the leaders of the Spanish Navy a massive headache. After a decade in development and billions of dollars spent, the Spanish Navy readied to unveil its newest submarine to the world in 2013—a triumph!—only to embarrassingly discover that it was 70 tons heavier than it should've been!

In other words, if the submarine had been tested in the water, it would've submerged and never returned to the surface. Yikes! And what turned this latest, cutting-edge vessel into a paper weight? Someone moved a decimal to the wrong spot during calculations, and no one caught it until the submarine had been built. Small things matter.

Here's one more for you.

Did you know that on January 31, 2009, for about an hour, Google broke the internet? Yes, *the internet!* Apparently, someone in Google accidentally added the forward slash (/) to a list of dangerous websites, and what do website addresses have in them? That's right, the forward slash!

On that January morning, millions of people tried to view websites and were redirected by their browsers to a site that itself crashed from the overload of traffic! Instead of the news or weather or sports scores or pictures of cats, everyone just stared at a blank screen.

To their credit, Google engineers figured out the problem very quickly and fixed it. But once again, we see that small things matter!

The Power of 1%

If small errors could lead to a satellite burning up, a submarine that just sinks, and the breaking of the internet, what could small, *positive* changes make in our lives?

Some years ago, I applied that very line of thinking to my life. At the time, I wasn't writing much, wasn't eating a very healthy diet, and wasn't exercising regularly. But then I decided that I would start changing myself for the better, 1% at a time.

Up to that point, I had sadly learned that trying to change 99% of yourself is about as successful as making New Year's resolutions: It doesn't work! The task is way too huge for anyone to pull off. But, think about 1%. *Anyone* can change 1% about themselves each year.

And that's what I started doing in my life. Each year, I pick something to improve about myself and continue this change throughout the year. The following year, I don't stop the 1% I've improved. I keep doing that 1% and add a new 1% to my life.

For example, one year my 1% was to start writing for 30 minutes a day, at least four days a week. And thanks to this decision, this will be the fourth book I've written—from a guy whose English teachers would have laughed if you even suggested I'd write *one* book in my life!

Small things matter.

Another year, I decided my 1% would be substituting grilled chicken for fried chicken in most of my meals throughout the week. Another 1% was exercising regularly. Another was cutting back on caffeine and sugar. And two years ago, I decided to floss my teeth every night before bed.

You see, 1% improvements in your life are doable, and they really don't seem like much once they become part of your daily routine. But over time, as long as you keep doing them, they'll stack up to some amazing benefits in your life!

So, stop for a minute and think about something that's small and positive that you could *change* about your life. What needs to change?

Small things matter!

Attitude of Gratitude

At the end of last year, I took a deep look at my life, I asked myself what I wanted to change. And you know what, I discovered that I can be rather ungrateful at times. I pray daily and thank God for his blessings, but I've realized that I lose sight of *most* of the things that God blesses with me each day of the year. I needed a better way to express my gratitude to God *and* to people.

So for this year's 1% positive change, I've chosen to keep a gratitude journal. Each day, every day, I write what I'm grateful for from that day. I can write a page or a paragraph or *one sentence*, but the key is writing down *something* that I'm grateful for. And let me tell you, it's been an eye-opener for me!

Through this gratitude journal, I've learned that something in my life was killing my joy.

Something has been dogging me with misery for my whole life; something has been casting a cloud over every sunny day of my life. And there's a good chance that it's been secretly draining the joy out of your life as well.

This joy-killer is *complaining*, and it's not new to humanity. It's been with us since Adam and Eve were expelled from the Garden of Eden, and chances are high that you may have complained about something to someone today. Maybe even just an hour ago!

Who Are These People?

Let me be the first to raise my hand and say, "Hi, my name is Jeff, and I struggle with complaining." And thinking back through my life, I can say that I've resembled all four of the following types of complainers. See if you resemble any of these:

> **The Whiner** — "Life's not fair. Everyone else gets all the good stuff."
>
> **The Martyr** — "No one appreciates me. I'm on my own."
>
> **The Cynic** — "Nothing will ever change. It's always going to be like this."
>
> **The Perfectionist** — "Nothing is right. Nothing is good enough."

Ever said or thought any of these things? I certainly have. Even reading them back to myself now, they can be so depressing. Statements like this said out loud or in our minds are like raining on a parade—actually, it's like us *causing* it to rain on *our* parade.

Complaining sours everything, from our relationships to our mood during the day to our outlook to our own future. And that's a powerful influence that we often miss, maybe because it's small stuff. But like I said before, small things matter.

In fact, complaining is so important that it is addressed in the Bible in Philippians 2:14-15:

Do everything without complaining or arguing, so that you may become blameless and pure, children of God without fault in a crooked and depraved generation, in which you shine like stars in the universe. (NIV)

I love these two verses because it doesn't just say, "Don't complain." It promises that if we don't complain, we will shine like stars! Let me tell you, in this dark world, full of negativity and depression, expressing gratitude and refraining from complaining sets us apart like blazing stars against the pitch-black tapestry of night! You can't get a stronger contrast.

Conquering Complaining

If you're like most people, complaining has become such a natural part of your life that you may not even realize you're doing it. It may be so routine with you that these negative phrases automatically fall from your mouth throughout the day.

But even if you don't realize it, I guarantee you that there are those around you who do know. You see, complaining is like bad breath: You don't know you have it, but everyone around you knows.

But there's hope!

Complaining is not invincible. It's not undefeatable. In fact, by applying the three concepts that follow to your daily thoughts and conversations, you can put yourself on the road to recovery from the gloom of complaining.

1. Admit you have a complaining problem

Admitting that we have a problem is always the place to start when something is a problem in our lives. It may seem obvious, yet the vast majority of people in the world that struggle with something haven't even gotten to this step. They just stay stuck in their problems.

Once you confront and admit the fact that you have a problem, you can now start working on changing yourself.

One time, a friend of mine bought a boat. He asked me to go with him to try it out and see what I thought about it. We got in the boat, started it up and took off. As we cruised along the lake, everything was fine at first.

But then I noticed that the boat seemed to be slowing down. I looked back to the rear of the boat, where the outboard motor was connected, and to my unhappy surprise, water was coming into the boat!

I shouted to my friend about the water and pointed to the back, but he just waved me off.

But then, we started slowing further, and my friend finally took notice. Now, more water was coming in and at a faster rate! Something had to change because we were too far from the shore to make it back before the boat was completely waterlogged.

My friend throttled back the engine, and I grabbed a plastic Solo cup, the only thing that would hold water, and started bailing as quickly as I could. Meanwhile, my buddy examined the back of the boat, trying to find how the water was getting in.

I was tossing water out of the boat as fast as I could, but more water was coming in!

Suddenly, my friend exclaimed something I won't put in here as he discovered the problem. There was a drain in the back of the boat that is supposed to be plugged before putting the boat in the water, and we hadn't plugged it.

With a shake of his head, my friend put the plug in, and we both bailed with our cups until we got the water level down to leave just a little water sloshing around in the floorboard.

Thankfully our adventure ended well. But first, we had to admit that there was a problem and change our actions in order to solve the problem.

Consider what Proverbs 28:13 says:

> A man who refuses to admit his mistakes can never be successful. But if he confesses and forsakes them, he gets another chance. (TLB)

Conquering complaining begins with admitting.

2. Realize that complaining is a warning sign

Have you ever been driving your vehicle when suddenly the fuel light came on? If you're like me, you probably think, "I just got gas! How is this empty already?"

That warning light is sending you a message, and you can choose not to heed it. But if you do, I hope you brought a good pair of walking shoes and an empty gas can.

In similar fashion, complaining can be a warning sign that something else is going on inside of you that needs to be addressed. If you don't like what you're seeing, watch what you're saying.

Ephesians 4:29 counsels:

> Do not let any unwholesome talk come out of your
> mouths, but only what is helpful for building others
> up according to their needs, that it may benefit those
> who listen. (NIV)

One of the best ways to combat complaining is to practice speaking positively by speaking words of encouragement to ourselves and others. Every time you want to complain, replace whatever you were going to say with something positive, uplifting, or encouraging. It can change the whole mood of your mind and the feel of a conversation!

3.   Switch to an Attitude of Gratitude

Deeper than just swapping out a complaint for a positive statement, switching to an attitude of gratitude is developing a whole new positive mindset that you live in daily. Instead of going through your day, identifying everything that goes wrong or not as expected, an attitude of gratitude looks at the world from a *thank-you-God* perspective.

But how can we develop a perspective of gratitude?

1 Thessalonians 5:16-18 gives us some specific steps to reach that goal. Take a look:

Be joyful; pray continually; give thanks in all circumstances, for this is God's will for you in Christ Jesus. (NIV)

I like to say, "A prayer-filled mind is a peace-filled heart." Prayer is a powerful way to rid your mind of anxiety and fear. Remember that trying to control what we cannot control raises anxiety within us. Instead, letting go of these things to God, reduces our stress.

Consider Philippians 4:6-7:

Do not be anxious about anything, but in everything, by prayer and petition, with thanksgiving, present your requests to God. And the peace of God, which transcends all understanding, will guard your hearts and your minds in Christ Jesus. (NIV)

Being joyful, praying throughout the day, and giving thanks despite circumstances are the supplies we need to plant a garden of gratitude in our mind. I find it interesting that these three things connect together so well: joy, prayer, giving thanks.

You might be wondering, "How do I pray continually? I have to work; I can't be on my knees 24 hours a day praying."

I'm glad you brought that up. *Praying continually* is not describing a physical act of unending prayer. Praying continually is a mindset that is open to God, thinking about God, and speaking to God throughout the day. You can pray out loud to God at times, pray in your mind at times, and other times, just sit in silence thinking about what he has done for you.

Hopefully, now you can see how prayer and giving thanks connect to give joy and create an attitude of gratitude.

This Just In!

Now let's look at the flipside. Complaining can turn us into an ungrateful person and eventually a hateful person. For years, I watched cable news in the morning and evening and listened to talk radio as I drove around town. And the whole time, all that was pumped into my ears and eyes was negativity and fear.

The news stories always sounded so dramatic, like at any moment something really horrible was about to happen or was happening. Doom, gloom, and the end of the world were the norm. Filling myself daily with this perspective on life put me on edge, robbed me of peace, stoked fear, and countered the joy of the Lord.

And when I turned all of that stuff off, I was amazed at how much peace and joy flooded back into my life. At first, I felt a little disconnected from the world, but in just a few weeks, I didn't miss all that negativity being pumped into my mind!

I challenge you to take a serious look at the media you're consuming each day, every day of the week. If you want to grow an attitude of gratitude, you're going to have to be choosy about what you feed your mind.

Go for the positive; nix the negative.

Back in the 80s

When I was a new Christian, I had an unrelenting hunger to learn more about God and the Bible. Unlike now, when there are countless

Bible studies available online or in apps, it was hard to find Bible study materials.

There were a few preachers on TV and radio, but if you didn't know what time their program came on and where to tune, you'd miss them. At the time, I didn't even know where to look.

One night, I was scanning through the radio channels on my big boom box, decked out with five speakers, AM, FM, and even short-wave radio, when I stumbled upon a man talking about Jesus. I thought, "Hey, this is just what I've been looking for!"

I made note of the radio dial setting, 91.5 FM, and the time, 9 PM, and I listened.

The preacher's name was Dr. Paul Walker, and at the time, he pastored a large church in the Atlanta area called Mount Paran. Every night, a different sermon of his was played, and I started consuming them.

I would sit on my bed, amazed at how much of the Bible this man could quote from memory. One time I counted, and he rattled off over fifty scriptures in just one message! Needless to say, this preacher became like a rock star to me.

A few years later, I had the privilege to meet Dr. Walker at a conference, where he shared a very personal story about being thankful *in* all circumstances and not *for* all circumstances. I'll never forget how his true story changed the way I thought about gratitude.

You Only Get One Life

Of Dr. Walker's two sons, Paul Dana Walker was the older. At Lee University, where he attended, Paul Dana was an excellent, popular athlete. He helped lead the basketball team to a 21-game win season. He also held the school record of 746 assists in 113 games. And when basketball season was over, he switched to pitching for the school's baseball team and ran cross country.

He also traveled, preaching at churches all over. His friend David Cooper—who is now Dr. Cooper and lead pastor of the Mount Paran Church—would ride along with him on these preaching trips, and the two of them would take turns preaching, one on Sunday morning and the other on Sunday night.

Paul Dana Walker was a devout follower of Jesus, and his life was a constant testimony about his love for God. He was loved by many, including his family. His father, Dr. Walker, was so thrilled that his son was taking after him in the ministry that he envisioned a time when he and his son would both pastor churches.

Then one night, Dr. Walker received a call late in the night. After picking up the receiver and greeting the person on the other, Dr. Walker listened and then shook his head in disbelief at what the person on the other end was saying. The man repeated the tragic news, and Dr. Walker dropped the phone receiver in horrified shock.

Paul Dana Walker and his wife, Julie, were traveling home after attending a Homecoming game at Lee, when they were involved in a fatal car accident. Paul died at the scene, and Julie sustained severe injuries to her body.

The loss of anyone we love is devastating, but the loss of a child, no matter what age, is gut wrenching to a parent.

Dr. Walker shared that the next days were just a blur. Even as he sat at a table at the funeral home making arrangements for his son's funeral, he couldn't believe that his son was actually gone. And in those moments when he was able to see that his death was real, I'm sure that he was filled with anger toward God and would ask, "Why, God? Why? How could you let this happen?"

But Dr. Walker was a man who loved God dearly, and he turned to God for strength and peace during the turmoil of this tragedy. During the funeral, Dr. Walker's wife, Carmelita, sang the song "God Is So Good," testifying to their family's belief that we should give thanks in all circumstances, no matter how awful, unfair, and undeserved they are. Despite anything and everything that happens, we put our trust in God.

You may have experienced a tragedy in your life that still haunts you, and when you think about it, you wonder, "Why, God? Why?"

I want to encourage you: You can find healing in giving your deep pain over to God. He loves you and wants to spend time with you as you share with him about the pain you carry.

For all of us, remember that we only get one life to live on this planet. What are you doing with yours?

An even better question for all of us is, "What would you like to do with yours?"

You see, my friend, if you're reading this, you still have a chance to make changes to your life to live a life that will leave you with no regrets when it comes your time to leave this world. I want you to really think hard and long on this following question: What would I like to do with the rest of my life?

I encourage you to use the principles found in this book to help you change the course of your life:

> You can make yourself better 1% at a time.
> You can grow by seeking out learning from the right *who*.
> You can take on the attitude of gratitude and live in a
> mindset of joy.
> You can lower your expectations on people and raise your expec-
> tations on God.

You can grow patience and the other fruits of the Spirit in your life.

You can let go of what you've been holding against others.

You can put your trust in God even when it seems like all of Hell is attacking you.

You can stop putting off what you've been putting off.

You CAN change your life!

Making It Personal

1. Using the 1% Principle to improve yourself slowly but consistently over time can stack up to some amazing results over the length of your life. What is a small 1% change that you could start doing today that would benefit you?

2. Of the following negative personality attitudes, which one do you have the most issue sounding and thinking like?

   The Whiner: "Life's not fair. Everyone else gets all the good stuff."

   The Martyr: "No one appreciates me. I'm on my own."

   The Cynic: "Nothing will ever change. It's always going to be like this."

   The Perfectionist: "Nothing is right. Nothing is good enough."

3. Read Philippians 2:14-15. In your own words, what is this verse saying to you?

4. If you are used to complaining, what are some steps that you can take to break yourself from this habit?

5. Since we are bombarded with negativity from all kinds of media every day, it can be easy to develop a sour outlook on life. Instead, how can we develop a perspective of gratitude to accentuate the positive in our life?

6. Read 1 Thessalonians 5:18. What is the difference between giving thanks *in* all circumstances and giving thanks *for* all circumstances?

7. CHALLENGE: Start a gratitude journal. It can be any kind of bound notebook. All you have to do is write a simple sentence in it each day, giving thanks to God for something from that day. Keep this gratitude journal in plain sight so that you will remember to write in it when you see it and keep your entries short so that you do not overwhelm yourself with lengthy writing. I promise you that when you look back over what God has done for you over the weeks, it will encourage you and fill you with an attitude of gratitude!